The Official
Arsenal
Dream Team

by

Adam Ward and Dave Smith

hamlyn

First published in Great Britain in 2003 by
Hamlyn, a division of Octopus Publishing Group Ltd
2–4 Heron Quays, London E14 4JP

ISBN 0 600 60834 4

A CIP catalogue record for this book is available from the British Library

Printed and bound in Italy

10 9 8 7 6 5 4 3 2 1

Note
The team chosen in this book is the result of an independent poll
conducted by the publishers and in no way constitutes the opinion
of Arsenal Football Club plc.

All records and statistics are correct up to May 2003

contents

Foreword
by Liam Brady

I have been proud to be associated, both as a player and now as Head of Youth Development, with Arsenal – a thoroughly professional football club steeped in history and one which continues to uphold the finest traditions which have made the Gunners great over many decades.

Liam Brady takes the fight to Leeds United.

Arsenal have been at the forefront of English football ever since the success of the 1930s when they were all-powerful. From the board down, the Club has continued to maintain those great traditions of excellence and do so with a touch of class and no shortage of style.

Even during the periods when the Club was not so successful – during the 1950s and 1960s – the same principles which had made Arsenal a force to be reckoned with were maintained and, in time, led to the Club getting back on the success trail with the Fairs Cup triumph of 1970 and, of course, the League and FA Cup 'double' the following year.

Whilst I was only able to claim an FA Cup winners' medal during my happy time as a player at Highbury, I have been delighted and proud to see the Club become established as the only team in the south of England to resist the power and might of Liverpool, during the 1970s and 1980s, and Manchester United in more recent times. The people who have run the Club must take enormous credit for that.

To win two 'doubles' under Arsène Wenger and two Championships under George Graham proves my point.

Now the plan has to be that we stay at the forefront of English football for years to come and impose ourselves in Europe. To really break into the big time on the continent means winning the Champions League, and that is what the Club is working towards. That is the ultimate goal.

A number of the players who have been trying to make that breakthrough in recent years are included in this *Arsenal Dream Team*, for which I am honoured to have been named too. Many other great players, a number of which I played alongside during my spell as a player between 1973 and 1980, have not been selected but, as we always say, football is a game of opinions.

I was fortunate to play with some colossal footballers and characters in the 1970s and working with the likes of Frank McLintock, Bob Wilson, Peter Simpson, John Radford, Ray Kennedy and many others as a youngster learning my trade certainly helped me develop as a player. I doubt I could have had a better grounding and the progress I made in the company of such footballing legends more than justified my decision to join the Club as a schoolboy.

Whilst it is always difficult to single out individuals when assessing Arsenal greats, because there have been so many, in my view one of the greatest players to have graced an Arsenal shirt is a player who didn't make this Dream Team...Alan Ball; my mentor as a youngster just breaking into the first team and a player I had so much respect for.

It is a shame that his time at the Club did not coincide with any great success, in terms of trophies won, and hence he might be forgotten by some as one of the great Arsenal players. Not by me. He was a big influence on me and, as a footballer, he was up there alongside the very best and he would certainly be in my Dream Team. But, again, it's all about opinions, isn't it and that's the beauty of books like this.

Looking at the midfield selections, I think the combination of myself and Patrick Vieira in the middle with David Rocastle and Robert Pires out wide would complement itself nicely. There's a good balance to it, and I'm sure I would have enjoyed playing alongside such an athlete as Patrick. I also think that Alan Ball for Patrick, George Armstrong for 'Rocky' and Graham Rix for Pires would have worked too.

So many great players and so many great memories for me as I look back on my playing career. I remember with great affection too how I was treated as a schoolboy when I first arrived at the Club; how friendly everyone was and how well they looked after the young players. Those things, as well as the prospect of working with some of the biggest names in the game, convinced me that Arsenal would be the best Club at which to start my career. I was right.

The fact that my teenage years as an Arsenal player were so enjoyable and rewarding, was also influential in my return to the Club as Head of Youth Development in 1996. I wanted to put something back into the Club at that level and, hopefully, provide the young players of today with the same opportunity I had to learn their trade in a wonderful and progressive environment.

We have some excellent players coming through the ranks, really top-notch footballers who I'm sure are going to go all the way in the game. Who knows, maybe in ten years time when another *Arsenal Dream Team* book is being put together, they will figure in the all-time XI.

Liam Brady

Liam Brady strides forward with Valencia's Mario Kempes in pursuit, 1981 Cup Winners' Cup final.

Introduction
by Adam Ward

There are some football clubs, naming no names, whose greatest team would pick itself. Arsenal is not one of those. The choices are seemingly endless: with a succession of top-quality players in each position, even before you consider the likes of Dennis Bergkamp and Charlie George who defy traditional definitions of striker or midfielder.

Who do you pick? The dilemmas are infinite: Kenny Sansom or Nigel Winterburn, Ian Wright or Thierry Henry, David O'Leary or Tony Adams. Selecting Arsenal's ultimate Dream Team is not an easy task. But thankfully it was one that hundreds of the Club's fans relished, judging from the poll conducted for this book.

The idea behind the book was to take the intriguing concept of the dream team selection, which has long been a staple feature of football autobiographies, and give the Club's fans the chance to have their say. It's a game many of us has played before, comparing players past and present and formulating fantasy Arsenal line-ups. What this book has done is provide an opportunity for the supporters to reach a consensus on the greatest Arsenal XI.

Advertisements appeared in the Club programme and magazine and on the official website, and many hundreds of supporters voted either by post or e-mail, selecting their teams in a 4–4–2 formation and also choosing their favourite manager, goals and games. Some of the players selected were foregone conclusions, others are more surprising. Tony Adams, inevitably, was in more people's teams than any other player, while Patrick Vieira was the second most popular choice.

One particularly interesting feature of the voting was that Arsenal fans were not preoccupied with current stars. Several players who took part in the 1970/71 'double' success received significant numbers of votes, demonstrating that Gunners fans are both loyal and knowledgeable.

We considered restricting the voting to players from the modern era, but it soon became apparent that many supporters had not forgotten the stars of the 1930s who played such a huge part in making Arsenal the institution it is today. So, alongside current players like Ashley Cole and Robert Pires you will find men like Cliff Bastin, Herbie Roberts and Alex James. There is little doubt that these heroes of Highbury past deserve their place in a book of this kind.

With the votes counted and the team chosen, we set about trying to understand the careers of the 11 men selected, along with a host of other contenders. Wherever possible we have spoken to team-mates and former coaches of the winning players, combining anecdotes with career details in an effort to create a true portrait of Arsenal's greatest XI.

Interviewing the likes of Viv Anderson, Bob Wilson, Paul Davis and Michael Thomas was truly a pleasure, and their illuminating tales of Highbury past have added much colour to this publication. It was particularly pleasing to talk to Thomas, whose goal against Liverpool in 1989 is undeniably the single most memorable in the Club's history.

You will notice that sometimes players have played in a variety of positions, and you may disagree with their inclusion in particular chapters, for example Frank McLintock is included in the team as a centre half but played much of his Arsenal career as a wing half. We have made our decision simply on the basis of the votes cast; that is to say, Frank was included in most people's teams as a defender rather than a midfielder.

Similarly, chapters do not always correspond with the shirt numbers generally worn by particular players, especially in regard to recent stars who have played in squad numbers. Thierry Henry, for example, wears 14 but is included in chapter 10. In most cases common sense dictates what chapter a player should be included in.

But whether you agree with where each player appears or not, one thing that is unarguable is that the XI selected for this book is truly a Dream Team.

Adam Ward
May 2003

Highbury hero: Arsenal fans celebrate a goal from Thierry Henry in 2002/03.

David Seaman FACTFILE

405 Appearances

0 Goals

Born: Rotherham, 19 September 1963
Joined Arsenal from Queens Park
Rangers in May 1990

Honours: League Championship
1990/91, 1997/98, 2001/02; FA Cup
1993, 1998, 2002, 2003; Coca-Cola Cup
1993; European Cup Winners' Cup 1994
International Honours: 75 England caps

'Lombardo hit the ball hard and toward the corner, but David showed **extraordinary anticipation**. It was a wonderful stop.'

Bob Wilson on Seaman's crucial penalty save against Sampdoria in the 1995 Cup Winners' Cup

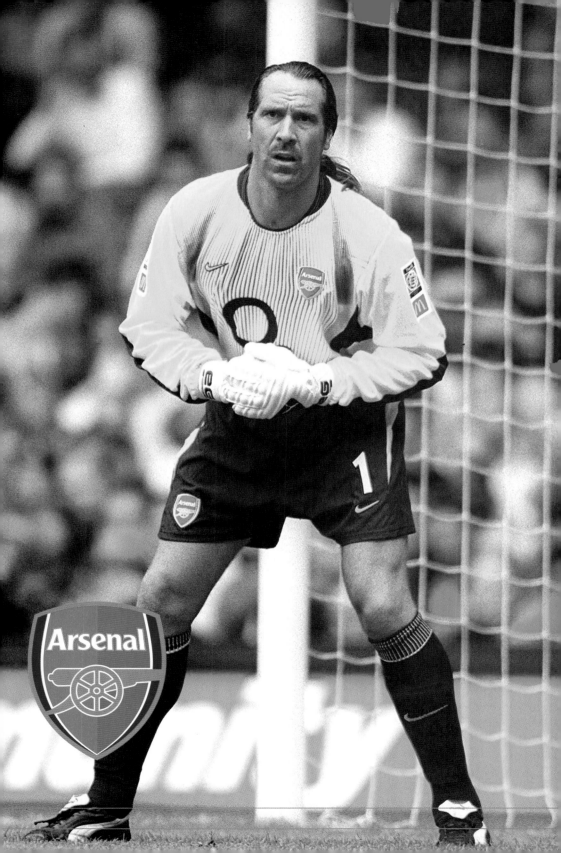

'You're not even taking a risk,' was the verdict of goalkeeping coach Bob Wilson when Arsenal manager George Graham told him he was thinking of making a substantial bid for Queens Park Rangers goalkeeper David Seaman in the summer of 1990. Thirteen years on, Wilson's judgement has been proved astute. Seaman has amassed an unrivalled collection of trophies, played more than 500 games for Arsenal and established a reputation as the greatest goalkeeper in the Club's history.

Wilson was unsurprised about David's inclusion in the Arsenal Dream Team. 'He has to be the choice as Arsenal's number one, in every respect,' he began. 'He's now topped 1,000 games, he's achieved so much and done it in great style. That was one of the nice things about the save he made from Paul Peschisolido's header in the FA Cup semi-final against Sheffield United. Instead of his career coming to a faltering end and people remembering Ronaldinho's free-kick in the World Cup and dredging up Nayim's goal – these freaky goals – he pulled off a save that ranks alongside Banks's stop against Brazil in 1970. Now, whenever he does retire, people will say we saw one of the greatest goalkeepers there's ever been. And that's what he is.'

Gordon Banks himself was generous in his praise of Seaman's save against Sheffield United. 'You would have to put this one by David in the same category as mine against Pelé in 1970,' said the former England keeper. 'The great thing with David's save is that he had all his weight on the wrong foot. He had to shift his weight on to the other foot and then get right across his goal. Then he didn't just block the ball with his arm, he scooped it away, which was crucial. For any goalkeeper it would have been an outstanding save but at the age of 39 it is quite remarkable. Good luck to David.'

Banks's praise is a massive tribute for Seaman, but nobody is better qualified to judge the relative merits of Arsenal's keepers than Bob Wilson, who has coached both John Lukic and Seaman and was himself the custodian during the 1970/71 'double' season.

> You would have to put this one by David in the same category as mine against Pelé in 1970.

Gordon Banks on Seaman's save against Sheffield United in April 2003

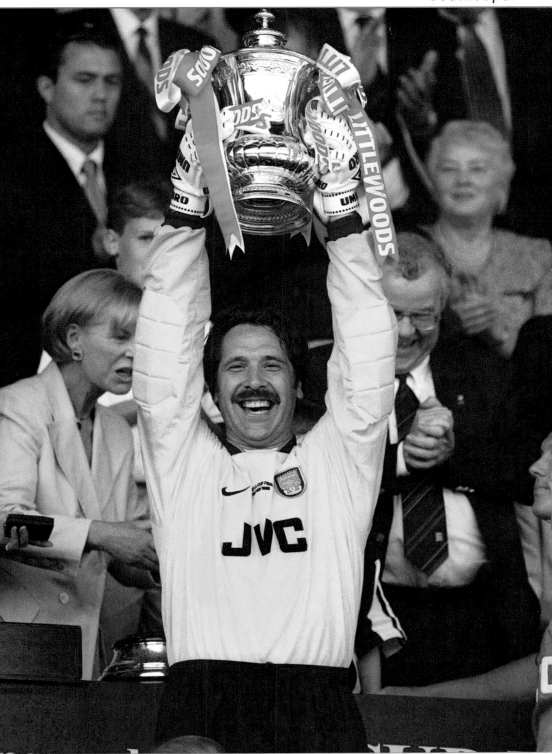

David lifts the FA Cup in 1998. It was the second of four Cup wins for the Yorkshireman.

Before Nayim scored that incredible goal, David had made a fantastic double save.

Bob Wilson

Of course, having spent the last 15 years as David's coach, he could be accused of bias, but the statistics and medals bear out Wilson's view of his protégé.

The two had been working together at QPR for the better part of four years when the move to Highbury came about. 'I knew exactly what Arsenal were getting,' explains Wilson. 'Mind you, David had already made the full England squad so George definitely wasn't taking a gamble. It was just a question of whether he could fulfil the potential he was showing, and he's not just done that, he's surpassed it. If you look at what he's won, all the League Championships, Cups and European finals, he's been an unbelievable signing.'

So what are David's strengths as a goalkeeper? Wilson offers a comparison with another of Arsenal's greatest keepers, Pat Jennings. 'David is as close to Pat Jennings as anyone I've seen, both in terms of presence and ability, and he has surpassed Pat in certain areas. He has superior overall technique but neither are chancers; they read the game well and play percentages. They assess situations and invariably know what is going to happen. Yes, of course they'll occasionally be beaten, and they're both horrified about that.'

Seaman's first season ended with Arsenal as champions, having conceded just 17 goals and lost one game. A defensive record of this kind is, of course, not solely the result of one man's good form but David's arrival had been the only personnel change in the team's backline since the previous season, which had seen Arsenal concede 38 goals and lose 12 games.

The only low point in an otherwise immaculate debut campaign came in the FA Cup semi-final defeat to Spurs at Wembley, in which David was beaten by a long-distance Paul Gascoigne free-kick. It was the first time he had faced vociferous media criticism but, as he has throughout his career, David paid no attention to the pundits and proved his character by helping Arsenal remain unbeaten for the remainder of the season.

A rare trophyless season followed the success of 1990/91 but the drought was only temporary, and in 1993 David completed a trio of domestic medals when he starred in FA Cup and League Cup final victories over Sheffield Wednesday. Better was to follow in 1993/94 when Arsenal won the Cup Winners' Cup, their first European trophy for 24 years, with George Graham's team conceding just three goals in nine matches.

'One-nil to the Arsenal' became a familiar chant at Highbury following the march to the Cup Winners' Cup final in Copenhagen, and David Seaman's contribution to the achievement was massive. Clean sheets in both legs of the quarter-final against Torino were followed by excellent performances in the semi-final against Paris St Germain, which Arsenal won 2–1 on aggregate. However, it was the final itself that saw David give one of his greatest performances in Arsenal colours. The Gunners were up against a Parma forward line that boasted Faustino Asprilla, Tomas Brolin and Gianfranco Zola.

All three were in their prime and were ably backed up by a strong supporting cast, but no Parma player could find a way past Arsenal's number one despite the fact that he played with a troublesome rib injury that restricted his mobility.

The defence of the Cup Winners' Cup in 1994/95 brought David highs and lows in equal measure. 'Before Nayim scored that incredible goal, David had made a fantastic double save from Zaragoza striker Juan Esnaider,' remembers Wilson. 'The forward shot from close range, but David went full length to tip the ball away. Then he recovered to keep out the rebound.'

Seaman had also played his part in Arsenal's progress to the final, never more so than in the semi-final against Sampdoria, which was decided by a penalty shoot-out. David saved three of the five penalties he faced, and it was the decisive spot-kick from Italian international Attilio Lombardo that was most impressive. 'Lombardo hit the ball hard and toward the corner, but David showed extraordinary anticipation. It was a wonderful stop,' remembers Wilson.

After the departure of George Graham in 1995, however, Arsenal finished only 12th in the Premiership having been unable to make a concerted challenge for the title since 1991. There were obvious weaknesses in the team, but with Ian Wright scoring goals and the legendary back four afforded even more security by Seaman's presence, the team's decline was not always apparent.

At international level, at least, David's career continued to progress and by the mid-1990s he was established as the national team's first-choice keeper. A string of

David saves Lombardo's penalty in the Cup Winners' Cup semi-final of 1995.

> David had no trouble adjusting to the backpass rule because he's so good with his feet.

Bob Wilson

top-class performances at the 1996 European Championships cemented his place in the hearts of England fans, with his penalty saves against Scotland and Spain catching the eye in particular. Unsurprisingly, David returned to Highbury full of confidence ahead of the 1996/97 campaign and soon afterwards found himself working under a manager who would give him the support and encouragement that would help him to fulfil yet more ambitions at club level. The arrival of Arsène Wenger at Arsenal in the autumn of 1996 brought the introduction of a host of progressive and modern ideas, many of which helped senior professionals like Tony Adams and David retain peak form for longer than might otherwise have been expected.

Under Wenger's tutelage David played in two 'double'-winning teams and added a host of other honours to his record. The manager himself describes his goalkeeper as 'an example of professionalism, particularly to young goalkeepers', adding that 'He's certainly fitter than when I arrived. He works much harder, has lost some weight and he puts more effort into training, maybe because he's intelligent enough to see he has to put more in to stay at this level when it was natural before.'

Bob Wilson is quick to point out that the keeper is also a versatile sportsman, as he proved when the rules of the game were changed to prevent goalkeepers picking up backpasses. 'David had no trouble adjusting to the backpass rule because he's so good with his feet, he's such a natural sportsman. He's got a great first touch and he's got an amazing calm about him. He's a great cricketer, a great snooker player and he can play outfield as well as in goal... and he's a brilliant fisherman! He's competitive at everything, he wants to win whatever he's doing.'

The poll for this book was one competition which David Seaman always looked sure to win. 'I'm just thrilled that it's David as I think fans are great judges,' says Wilson, before adding, 'And let's not forget that goalkeeping has never been more difficult than it is now.' Wilson is undoubtedly right, but one Yorkshireman has a knack of making it look easy.

David shows his delight after the 2–0 win at Old Trafford in the FA Cup, February 2003.

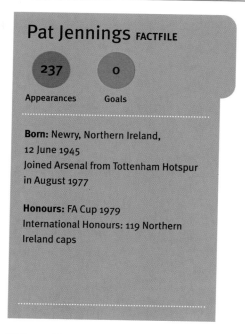

Pat Jennings FACTFILE

237 Appearances

0 Goals

Born: Newry, Northern Ireland,
12 June 1945
Joined Arsenal from Tottenham Hotspur
in August 1977

Honours: FA Cup 1979
International Honours: 119 Northern
Ireland caps

> You would think "It's OK, Pat'll save it." And invariably he did.
>
> Viv Anderson

The Runner-up

'Good morning God,' was how Arsenal's players greeted goalkeeper Pat Jennings during the giant Irishman's reign as the team's undisputed number one in the 1970s and 1980s. 'In my eyes, and those of most of the pros at the Club at the time, he was "God",' remembers Viv Anderson. 'That is how much respect he carried within the squad. With everyone.' The Arsenal fans shared the players' adoration for Jennings, who was signed from rivals Tottenham Hotspur in 1977.

The nature of Pat's signing in fact did much to endear him to the Highbury faithful. He was one of three men to make the switch from White Hart Lane, with manager Terry Neill the first, swiftly followed by Willie Young and then Pat. At the age of 32, the genial keeper was considered past his best by Spurs boss Keith Burkinshaw who accepted a transfer bid from Neill in the summer of 1977. Jennings, however, played on for another seven seasons, making 326 appearances for Arsenal before retiring in 1985. At this point he had won an FA Cup medal in 1979 and played in three other Cup finals.

Bob Wilson is in no doubt as to the quality of Jennings. 'Pat was one of the most natural goalkeepers I've ever seen in my life. He was natural from the point of view that he had an extraordinary, unique style. He was the first goalkeeper to save with his feet consistently; nowadays everybody saves with their feet but when I was playing nobody kicked the ball away on a regular basis.'

Jennings's physical size – he was an imposing six-footer – allied to his calm demeanour made him a formidable opponent but a reassuring presence to his team-mates. 'He had immense presence and nothing ever fazed him,' recalls Anderson. 'There was never any panic, never any rants or raves at his defenders if anything went wrong. He was as far removed as you could possibly get from the Peter Schmeichel type of keeper. Big Pat was an absolute joy to play with.'

His unique style was probably down to the fact that he was largely uncoached. 'Back then there was no specific goalkeeper training,' explains Wilson, 'instead all you had was shooting practice where a succession of shots were fired at you.' As a result, Pat evolved his own style, which reflected his calm and assured personality.

'There was an aura about Pat and it was one he created without having to say much,' explains Anderson. 'He was as quiet off the field as he was on it. When there was something to say he would say it, and it was always considered, not just blurted out in the heat of the moment. If you did make a mistake he would choose his moment to have a quiet word with you, take you to one side and tell you what he wanted you to do and where to go. He was a great pro.'

Pat's calm demeanour inspired confidence in those around him, and there is no doubt that his presence had a positive influence on morale. 'He oozed confidence and the composure he portrayed swept throughout the team, especially the back four,' recalls Anderson. 'I only played about 18 games with him before he left the Club, but even though he was approaching 40 at the

time he was still an exceptional keeper and I can only imagine what he must have been like in his prime.

'I have played with some great keepers in my time, such as Peter Shilton, Ray Clemence and Joe Corrigan, and Pat was right up there with the very best of them even at that late stage of his career. There was probably no one better in one-v-one situations and, as a defender, you always knew that if we had been exposed Big Pat was there to get you out of the mire. You would think "It's OK, Pat'll save it." And invariably he did. It was the same with Shilts when I was at Forest.'

It should also be remembered that Pat's time at Highbury coincided with a difficult era for the Club, and his record of just one major trophy (the 1979 FA Cup) does not reflect his achievements and the consistently high standard of goalkeeping he provided in almost eight years at Arsenal.

Pat Jennings sends a clearance forward in the 1979 FA Cup final. Joe Jordan looks on.

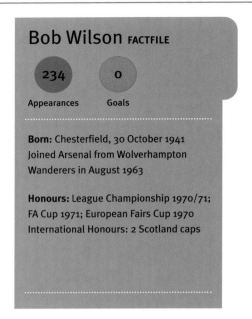

Bob Wilson FACTFILE

234
Appearances

0
Goals

Born: Chesterfield, 30 October 1941
Joined Arsenal from Wolverhampton
Wanderers in August 1963

Honours: League Championship 1970/71;
FA Cup 1971; European Fairs Cup 1970
International Honours: 2 Scotland caps

Third Place

**Bob Wilson took a somewhat convoluted
journey to Arsenal and professional football
via Loughborough College, Wolverhampton
Wanderers and a full-time teaching job before
establishing himself among the nation's leading
keepers.**

Although modest about his achievements, Bob
admits to feeling quietly proud of the fact that he
was the last amateur to establish himself as an
Arsenal player. 'I knew it would be difficult but I
was ambitious and it was a massive achievement.
It was also courageous of the manager, Billy
Wright, but all you can say is that he was
struggling for keepers.'

Several senior players offered Bob advice on
how to settle at the Club. 'Joe Baker would say to
me, "You're an amateur, you've missed all the
apprenticeships that the lads have come through
since the age of 15. You're breaking the mould, so
the first thing you've got to do is win their respect
and you can only do that by showing that you can
play,"' recalls Bob. 'He understood my frailty as an
amateur in a world of professionals; I'd turn up to
play from my job as a teacher at a school.'

Bob soon gained that respect, not least
because of his bravery. 'Speed of reaction and
speed of thought were the outstanding features of
my game and I had to be a gambler,' explains Bob.
'It's ironic that people look on me as being a calm
person because I was not a calm goalkeeper.

'I was quick on my feet and I had good hand-
eye co-ordination. I also had the ability, or
instinct, to dive headlong at the ball in one-v-ones
and in crowded penalty areas. I did pay a heavy
price for it though, and I ended up riddled with
injuries. But that was what lifted me out of the
ordinary. It was a daring style; it imitated my idol
Bert Trautmann and it was appreciated by the
crowd. People still say to me, "You're the most
courageous goalkeeper I've ever seen." I never
looked at it like that because it was natural
to me.'

By the late 1960s Bob had seen off the
challenge of Jim Furnell to make the number one
jersey his own. He helped Arsenal to the Fairs Cup
in 1969/70 before playing a full role in the 'double'
success a year later. Bob retired in 1974 but later
returned to the Club as goalkeeping coach.

A gloveless Bob Wilson takes to the field.

The Contenders

John Lukic, 1983–1990 and 1996–2001
(241 appearances, 0 goals)

His career sandwiched unenviably between those of Pat Jennings and David Seaman, John Lukic nevertheless helped Arsenal to their first League title for 18 years in 1988/89, offering an assured presence behind the newly formed defence of Winterburn, Dixon, Adams and Bould. 'John came into the side when Pat Jennings left about 16 games into the 1984/85 season,' remembers Viv Anderson. 'And even though he was replacing a legend he wasn't fazed. He had a good build for a keeper and he was never afraid to come for crosses. He was a good shot-stopper too.'

Bob Wilson is similarly positive about John's contribution to the Arsenal cause. 'Lukey was an extraordinary professional – one of the best I've ever worked with – and for his height he was so agile. He's the only keeper in the history of the game to win championships with two different clubs; after leaving Highbury, he won the title with Leeds in 1992.'

John returned to the Club in 1996 and Wilson is similarly effusive about the player's second spell. 'When he came back to the Club he was extraordinary in what he did as a number two. He was absolutely brilliant and people loved having him around.'

Jack Kelsey, 1951–1962
(327 appearances, 0 goals)

It is difficult to compare the careers of modern-day keepers with that of Jack Kelsey, the former Welsh steelworker who forged a reputation as Britain's greatest goalkeeper of the 1950s. In his era the rules of the game were different, charging and barging of goalkeepers was commonplace, the ball was heavy and pitches were quagmires. But in this physically demanding environment, the Swansea-born stopper had no equal.

Jack arrived at Highbury from amateur football. After a season spent on the fringes of the first team, Jack was given the chance to establish himself in the first team. It was the start of a ten-season run as Arsenal's first-choice 'keeper.

Jack was a formidable last line of defence. He was tall, strong and renowned for his ability to pluck crosses from the air and his calm, assured positioning. In a period when the team was of only moderate quality, Jack himself was undeniably world class. This fact was underlined by his performances for Wales, whom he helped progress to the last eight of the World Cup in 1958.

His first team position at Highbury was threatened briefly by a broken arm, but he was soon back as first-choice keeper until a back injury curtailed his career.

The ever-popular John Lukic in his second spell at Arsenal

Lee Dixon FACTFILE

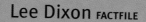

458 Appearances

25 Goals

Born: Manchester, 17 March 1964
Joined Arsenal from Stoke City in
January 1988

Honours: League Championship
1988/89, 1990/91, 1997/98, 2001/02;
FA Cup 1993, 1998, 2002; European Cup
Winners' Cup 1994
International Honours: 22 England caps

'I always made it abundantly clear to people that

Arsenal would be my last club.

I just didn't want to play for anyone else.'

Lee Dixon

Fittingly, Lee Dixon bowed out a 'double' winner, ending his Arsenal career at the age of 38 after more than 600 appearances in 14 years as a vital member of the defence on which the Club's success between 1989 and 2002 was built. If anyone deserved to go out at the very top it was the likeable, reliable and tireless Mancunian.

Few Arsenal managers could have conducted a better piece of transfer business than that which brought Dixon to Highbury from Stoke in January 1988 for a fee which the full back repaid many times over. Within two years he had won a Championship medal and earned England recognition, going on to gain 22 international caps.

Lee's attacking ability no doubt stemmed from his early days at Burnley. He began his career there as a winger, although he would soon make his name stopping wingers. As a defender he was competitive and dogged, strong in the air and blessed with a priceless positional awareness that rarely saw him caught out. At the other end of the field, Lee proved himself a potent outlet for the side, providing great service to the front men while having the speed to track back diligently.

Dixon won four League titles, three FA Cups and the European Cup Winners' Cup. He decided to retire after the 2002 'double' had been secured following a discussion with manager Arsène Wenger, a meeting he remembers with a tinge of sadness: 'I hadn't really made up my mind until Arsène Wenger called me into the office prior to training one day. It was the first time we had spoken about it. At the start of the season I had intimated that it would be my last, but because I was out for the first five and a half months through injury, my original plan was thrown into chaos.

'The fact that I hadn't missed selection in the squad since Christmas [2001] kept me going. However, the longer the season went on the more I realized I couldn't continue to play at the highest level for much longer. It was too much for my knee and ankle, but I needed someone who I totally respected to tell me it was time to call it a day. It needed someone with Arsène's intelligence and

> I want to win honours with Arsenal, then get myself noticed. It would be terrific to earn international recognition.

Lee Dixon in 1988

Lee holds aloft the Premiership trophy after the success of 1997/98.

know-how to push me over the edge. Arsène was very clear that the defenders he inherited at Arsenal had done well for him, and though it was an emotional decision, I was relieved my mind had been made up.'

Dixon admits that it hurt somewhat to be reminded that time had finally caught up with him, even though his exuberance and enthusiasm still knew no bounds. But at least he was walking away safe in the knowledge that he had gone out at the top and with his reputation firmly intact. He says: 'When we won the 'double' in 1998, I felt I had done well to be a part of the team, but to do it again four years later was the stuff of dreams. What better way to go out than collecting the 'double' trophies at Highbury? It was an outstanding season and brilliant to be a part of that squad – it was the best I've played with, with depth in every position.'

That depth meant, as Wenger had explained to him and Dixon came to accept, that his opportunities of first-team action would become increasingly rare. He didn't fancy fading into the background, he didn't want to overstay his welcome and, more importantly, he never considered the option of ending his career elsewhere. Once he'd made up his mind that he was going to retire at the end of the 2001/02 season, or had the decision made for him, he knew that was it. 'I knew that I would miss the game desperately when it all came to an end, but I always made it abundantly clear to people that Arsenal would be my last club. I just didn't want to play for anyone else.'

Having begun his career with Burnley, Dixon was released by the club in 1984 after making just a handful of first-team appearances. When he was later asked – in 1990, by which time he was an established Arsenal star – to write a short article about his time at Turf Moor for the Burnley programme, he described his rejection by the club as 'the saddest day of my professional career', adding: 'I was devastated to leave such a well-respected club as Burnley, but it was probably a blessing in disguise as it spurred me on to reach my goal of making it as a professional footballer.'

Lee bounced back, making steady progress with Chester and then Bury before joining Stoke in 1986. Two years later he was travelling down the motorway to meet George Graham to discuss the terms of his move to Arsenal, a meeting which was to change his life. His Highbury career began with a handful of first-team appearances towards the end of the 1987/88 season, making his debut in the 2–0 win against Luton on 13 February 1988, but by the start of the following campaign he was established as the first-choice right back – a position he was to hold for 14 years.

 I was rubbing the tears out of my eyes and hoping that the ball didn't come down my side because I wouldn't be able to see it!

Lee Dixon after Michael Thomas scored the goal that won Arsenal the 1989 title

An emotional Lee Dixon acknowledges the crowd during Tony Adams's testimonial match.

His dogged and determined defending, combined with his rampaging runs down the right flank, quickly established him as a fans' favourite, and he was a key member of the George Graham team that won the 1988/89 League title in dramatic fashion at Anfield. Dixon, who made 33 appearances that season and registered the first of his 28 Arsenal goals in a 2–0 win at home to Everton during the run-in, remembers that magical night on Merseyside well and his memories of Michael Thomas's winning goal – which he'd helped create with a ball played into Alan Smith – and the celebrations that followed are still vivid.

He recalls: 'I was still standing on the halfway line when Michael flicked the ball towards goal. I didn't actually see the ball cross the line but I saw Nigel [Winterburn] running across the goal with his arms up, so I thought that it must be in. I burst out crying on the halfway line. There was no one near me, so I ran back to John Lukic, who was standing on the edge of the box, saying, "I told you I should have thrown it to you." He just said, "Great ball." We were still hugging each other when I heard a whistle and Liverpool were kicking off again. I was rubbing the tears out of my eyes and hoping that the ball didn't come down my side because I wouldn't be able to see it! I don't know how long it was before the ref blew the final whistle, but it seemed like about three hours! That was a good dressing room afterwards!'

There were to be plenty more such scenes, the next occasion being just two years later when Arsenal celebrated regaining the League title in 1991. Lee was ever-present, scoring five vital goals all from the penalty spot. Two years on and Lee was collecting his first FA Cup winners' medal following the 1993 replay victory over Sheffield Wednesday, having earlier missed out on a League Cup winners' medal when he was absent through suspension for the Wembley final against the same opposition. He added a Cup Winners' Cup winners' medal to his collection the following season but then experienced a rare barren run of four years before the 'double' triumph of 1998.

The following year, after 11 seasons of sterling service, came Lee's well-deserved testimonial match against Real Madrid. It was supposed to be his big night but Ian Wright did his best to upstage the popular defender. The kick-off was delayed by 20 minutes because Wright, by that time with Celtic, had thrown the shirts of Marc Overmars and Davor Suker out of the Arsenal dressing room into the street and into the arms of delighted Arsenal fans. Kit man Vic Akers had to dash to the Arsenal Club shop to get replacement shirts and have them printed up with new names and numbers. Later in the evening, when Wright came on to replace Suker, the Club's record goalscorer received the loudest cheer of the night, leaving Dixon to joke: 'It was very nice for me to play in Ian Wright's testimonial!' It was Lee's night, though, and he played the whole game with a smile as wide as the North Bank, enjoying plenty of banter with the crowd of more than 22,000 who had turned up to salute his massive contribution to the Club's history. He even stopped at one point during the game to applaud them when the attendance was announced. It was typical of Dixon: always appreciative of others, fans and team-mates alike.

Despite the arrival of Oleg Luzhny and Lauren, Lee kept dashing up and down the right flank to great effect and only during his final season – 2001/02 – did a niggling knee injury begin to take its toll. So, with another League and Cup 'double' to his name, the curtain came down on a memorable career. Lee retired fourth in the all-time list of appearances for the Club after one last, emotional 90-minute performance in the final game of the season against Everton. That day Tony Adams lifted the trophy Arsenal had clinched just days before at Old Trafford, where Lee also made a fleeting appearance. There was one last swansong for Lee: after joining his team-mates on an open-top bus tour of North London to parade the latest additions to his and Arsenal's trophy collection, he appeared in Tony Adams's testimonial – and scored. It was an apt way to sign off.

Afterwards Lee said: 'I would like to take this opportunity – without getting too emotional – to thank all my team-mates over the last 13 or 14 years, all my managers, all the backroom staff who have helped me try to perform to the highest level, but most of all to all the fans. I would like personally to thank every one of you for supporting the Club and myself. I wouldn't have done any of this without you.' In return, manager Arsène Wenger paid tribute to Lee for his contribution: 'Lee has been a tremendous player and I hope that he stays in the game because he is a really strong character. What he has done for this Club is fantastic and he has been a tremendous servant.'

When we won the 'double' in 1998 I felt I had done well, but to do it again four years later was the stuff of dreams.

Lee Dixon

A tenacious Lee gets the better of Everton's Gary Naysmith.

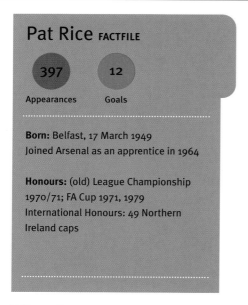

Pat Rice FACTFILE

397 Appearances

12 Goals

Born: Belfast, 17 March 1949
Joined Arsenal as an apprentice in 1964

Honours: (old) League Championship
1970/71; FA Cup 1971, 1979
International Honours: 49 Northern
Ireland caps

> ' I knew I wasn't expected to succeed. So I worked really hard at my game and eventually it paid off... '
>
> Pat Rice

The Runner-up

The phrase 'Arsenal through and through' could never be more appropriate than when used to describe Pat Rice, who has the distinction of being one of the few (Bob Wilson would be another) to have played a part in all three of the Club's 'double' triumphs; as a player in 1971 and assistant manager in 1998 and 2002.

Even when he was taken on as an apprentice in 1964, his commitment stood out, and what he lacked in certain aspects of the game he more than made up for in sheer determination. His willingness to learn and to develop as a player made him a regular and valuable member of the Arsenal first team for ten full seasons, latterly as captain.

As a result of the tireless work he put in on the training ground, improving his technique as a defender as well as his speed and awareness, Pat impressed enough to earn his place in the first-team squad and was identified as a 'winner' by manager Bertie Mee.

The young Irishman was a member of Arsenal's victorious FA Youth Cup-winning team in 1966 but he remembers that, 'the Club took a chance on me. There were many more naturally gifted players than

me in our 1966 Youth Cup-winning side. What kept me going was tremendous determination. I knew I wasn't expected to succeed. So I worked really hard at my game and eventually it paid off.'

Pat did not have to wait long for his chance. He made his debut during the 1969/70 season when Arsenal claimed the Fairs Cup as a prelude to their League Championship and FA Cup success. Peter Storey had been Arsenal's regular right back prior to the 'double' season, but when Storey moved into midfield, Pat had the chance to stake his claim to the number two jersey on a regular basis. Mee was quick to appreciate that Pat – like the solid Peter Simpson – offered the kind of defensive fortitude and reliability that was essential in a back-four that already boasted cavalier talents like Frank McLintock and Bob McNab. Pat used the ball constructively enough, but, in his early days at least, it was the defensive side of his game that caught the eye.

He missed only one League game during the 'double'-winning season, also playing in every FA Cup tie including the final against Liverpool, and was a permanent member of the team which defended its Fairs Cup title with pride before being defeated on the away goals rule by Cologne in the quarter-finals.

Pat's determination was vital during the 1971 FA Cup final. The pundits had expected him to be given a torrid afternoon by Liverpool's exciting young winger Steve Heighway. But, though the Liverpool man scored the game's opening goal, Pat was not held culpable and throughout the game he acquitted himself well.

Pat went on to play in a further five FA Cup finals for Arsenal, captaining the victorious 1979 team in a dramatic game against Manchester United. As he grew in experience and confidence, his game evolved, and by the late 1970s he was a more frequent participant in attacking play. However, his greatest contribution to the Gunners cause was as a leader.

Pat was appointed Club captain following the departure of Alan Ball in 1977 and his stoical presence was vital in a somewhat uncertain period at Highbury. Players came and went, managers did likewise, but Pat remained. It was particularly reassuring for young players like David O'Leary and Liam Brady to see such a consistent and dependable figure as Pat leading the team out.

After 11 years and 13 goals, Pat Rice finally called time on his playing career with Arsenal in 1980. He did not go far – only to Watford, where he enjoyed a successful four-year sojourn that took in a promotion and another Cup final. Within months of his departure from Watford, Pat had come back to his spiritual home of Highbury and he spent the next 12 seasons successfully nurturing Arsenal talent of the future as the Club's youth-team coach.

In 1996 he led his charges to FA Youth Cup success, 30 years after he had won the same competition as a player. However, he resisted the temptation to tell his players about the achievements of his own career. 'I'll never tell the lads about my achievements,' explained Pat. 'I'll offer advice gained from situations that have happened to me – but I'd hate to keep ramming my big moments down their throats. They'd soon get fed up and lose respect for me in the process.'

It is hard to imagine that anybody at Highbury could have anything but respect for a man who has served the Club so loyally both as a player and more recently as Arsène Wenger's assistant manager.

A typically impassioned Pat Rice urges his team-mates on.

The Contenders

Viv Anderson, 1984–87
(120 appearances, 9 goals)

Tall, quick, skilful and tenacious, Viv Anderson was a player of bountiful talent. As a defender his height and athleticism were of obvious benefit, but the same qualities, allied to an assured touch, made him an equally effective attacker. Viv's marauding bursts down the flank made him a persistent menace to opposing left backs, while his prodigious aerial ability made him no less of a nuisance to central defenders from set pieces.

Anderson arrived at Highbury from his home town club of Nottingham Forest as a 28-year-old with a reputation as one of the most accomplished defenders in English football. It was a reputation that could be backed up too, as during his time at Forest, he had amassed an impressive collection of trophies, which included two European Cups.

Viv, who had been the first black player to play for England, joined Arsenal in 1984. It was a move that reunited him with his former England coach

Don Howe. Viv signed a three-year contract and he says: 'I spoke to my old Forest pal Tony Woodcock and he told me good things about Arsenal so it seemed like the perfect move.'

Anderson quickly impressed the Highbury faithful with his adventurous fullback play. He would play 120 League games for Arsenal, collecting a League Cup medal in the process. One of the most impressive features of Viv's time as a Gunner was his appearance record. He barely missed a game in three seasons. 'I think one of the main reasons I got the move to Arsenal in the first place was because I didn't miss many games,' recalls Viv. 'I was fortunate that I never picked up any injuries.'

However, when his contract came to an end, Viv opted to join Manchester United. He had served the Club well and his presence had helped many emergent players, including Tony Adams. 'I had a great time at Arsenal... it's just a shame that, given the quality we had in that squad, we didn't win more than just that League Cup.'

Viv Anderson brought skill and experience to Arsenal's number two jersey in the 1980s.

Lauren has made an easy transition from midfielder to right back.

Lauren, 2000–present
(72 appearances, 5 goals)

Not much was known in English football about the versatile Cameroon international on his arrival at Highbury in the summer of 2000, although he had played with some distinction in Spain for a number of years before Arsène Wenger signed him from Real Mallorca. Yet within a year he had already proved his worth in more than one position.

Athletic and with boundless energy, Lauren quickly showed that he had no shortage of ability either. The fact that he was able to adapt rapidly to the pace and power of the English game as well as to a variety of positions made him a vital squad member and a hit with the fans, not least because of the goal he scored on his home debut – his first full appearance – in a 2–0 win over Liverpool.

Having arrived essentially as a right-sided midfielder, he proved himself equally adept in a variety of midfield roles, making 18 appearances in his first season. He began the 'double'-winning season at right back in place of the injured Lee Dixon. Lauren's versatility in playing at both midfield and right back was crucial to the team's success and his international class was further underlined by helping Cameroon reclaim the African Nations' Cup in the same season.

Lauren is clearly one of Arsenal's most consistent performers whether it's with pace, skilful attack or sharp, sensible defending.

Kenny Sansom FACTFILE

314
Appearances

6
Goals

Born: Camberwell, London, 26 September 1958
Joined Arsenal from Crystal Palace in August 1980

Honours: Littlewoods Cup 1987
International Honours: 86 England caps

'Kenny was so **quick** at **left back** he never had to be aggressive. The only player to read situations nearly as well as him was Paolo Maldini.'

Charlie Nicholas

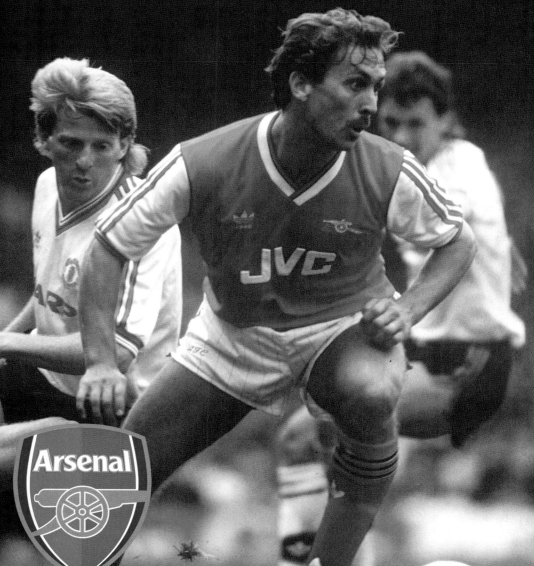

How good a player was Kenny Sansom? Well, no less an Arsenal authority than Charlie George rates him as the greatest left back in the Club's history. 'There wasn't much Kenny couldn't do on the field,' continues Charlie. 'He defended soundly, tackled crisply, distributed the ball intelligently, and got up to support the attack so he was the all-round package.' Voters in the poll for this book clearly concur with Charlie's view. However, it all might have been so different but for one of the most bizarre transfer deals ever, which brought Kenny to Highbury in the summer of 1980.

Terry Neill had been looking to inject new blood into his team following the departure of Liam Brady, and he began his close-season spending with the encouraging signing of Queens Park Rangers' exciting young striker Clive Allen for a Club record fee. However, before Allen could play a competitive game for his new club he found himself the subject of another record-breaking transfer. Neill had decided that he was happy with his front pairing of Frank Stapleton and Alan Sunderland. Clive was the odd man out. Within weeks he had joined Crystal Palace with Kenny moving in the opposite direction.

Arsenal fans were left perplexed. They had signed and sold a promising young striker and had ended up with a new left back, albeit a 21-year-old England international. However, any disappointment was soon replaced by optimism and excitement as the defender made his mark in an Arsenal jersey.

Sansom went straight into the first team for his Arsenal debut against West Brom and was an ever-present throughout the 1980/81 season. He hardly missed a game for the next seven years, successfully replacing the popular figure of Sammy Nelson. His England career also continued to flourish and he would win 86 caps, a record for a fullback.

'Kenny was small and squat, very quick too, and to get round him or past him was an achievement in itself.'

Viv Anderson

Kenny poses with the League Cup ahead of the 1987/88 season.

In his time at Palace, under Terry Venables, Kenny had already gained a reputation as an attacking fullback who was equally at home in the opposition's half of the field as he was in his own; happy to get forward in support of the midfield and front men at any given moment and with the speed and awareness to get back to perform his defensive duties. 'Kenny was so quick at left back he never had to be aggressive,' said former team-mate Charlie Nicholas.

Venables, who had handed Kenny his League debut as a 16-year-old, has no doubt as to Sansom's quality. 'He looked fantastic, but then after quite a few games he took a dip and we wondered whether he was going to be as good as we thought,' recalls the former Palace manager. 'But it was just a temporary thing because he then kicked on again. That often happens. You go up, then go off because it's a lot to handle, but then go again.'

Such was the impact Sansom made in his first season at Highbury that, by the end of it, he was voted the Club's player of the year by the supporters. The fans had been greatly impressed by his all-round ability – even in the air. At 5ft 8in he was by no means the tallest, but he won more than his fair share of aerial duels although he was most noted for his near-faultless first touch, his intelligent use of the ball and his unselfish support play.

Kenny was a modern fullback who was comfortable in possession and adventurous in his attacking play. Of course, there were some dour souls who argued that he left his fellow defenders exposed because of his eagerness to support the front players. With experience, however, which he was also gaining on the international stage, he soon mastered the art of when to go and when to stay, and he was a much more consistent performer once that aspect of his game was fully developed.

He wasn't a defender who favoured the lunging tackle, preferring instead to jockey his opponent away from the danger area before using his impeccable timing to make an interception at the vital moment. He wasn't often caught out and was rarely, if ever, given the runaround by even the liveliest of wide men. According to former right back Viv Anderson, who was to operate in tandem with his England colleague for three seasons at club level, 'He must have been a nightmare for wingers to play against.'

Anderson continues: 'Kenny was small and squat, very quick too, and to get round him or past him was an achievement in itself. Wingers rarely did, even those he came up against on the international stage, which is why he won 80-odd England caps. We both liked to get forward, but we wouldn't go gung-ho. If Kenny went on a run I would hold back and tuck in, and he would do likewise when I pushed on. He was an extra special player.'

 He was so solid, consistent, and always on top of his job.

Alan Ball

Kenny moves forward as Everton's Adrian Heath forlornly gives chase.

Sansom played in every one of Arsenal's 47 League and Cup games during the 1980/81 season, earning his first goal against Stoke in September and adding a couple more against Norwich and Ipswich later in the campaign which saw the Club finish third in the table, seven points behind champions Aston Villa. He had to wait a further three seasons for his next Arsenal goal, the glorious moment finally arriving on 14 January 1984 when he struck in a 2–1 win at Luton. However, in the interim, he remained a frequent contributor to Arsenal's attacking play, with his attacking forays and left wing centres providing a succession of assists for the strikers.

Kenny, whose career at Highbury coincided with a transitional period and the reigns of three managers, collected the first winners' medal of his Highbury career, for the Littlewoods Cup, as captain in 1987. Many lesser players have won more, but the Arsenal career of this legendary fullback cannot be judged purely in terms of silverware. His contribution was immense both on and off the field.

Don Howe had first made Kenny captain but it was under George Graham's tenure that he led the team out for the Wembley showdown with Liverpool in 1987. The match against Kenny Dalglish's team was decided by two goals from Charlie Nicholas, but the Scottish striker is fulsome in his praise of the man who held aloft the first trophy of Graham's reign. 'Kenny isn't that big but football is

Glenn Hoddle is beaten to the ball by a flying Sansom.

> ❛ There wasn't much Kenny couldn't do on the field... he was the all-round package. ❜

Charlie George

about tactics and ability not about being 6ft 5in' Charlie added: 'Kenny had quick feet, wingers' type of feet in terms of moving the ball. He made little short strides and you'd think you'd got him, then he would just ease away. And in the dressing room he was brilliant... a fabulous entertainer and a player who commanded respect from other pros.'

Kenny's leadership qualities are often underestimated, but he was undoubtedly valued by the players who took to the field behind him. Former team-mate Chris Whyte says: 'When you are in the spotlight all the time you have to be able to find that happy medium between a laugh and a joke and the serious business and Kenny was always spot on, very professional.'

Tony Adams has similar recollections of Kenny's ability to alleviate the dressing room tension prior to a match, and it is clear that the left back had a major influence on the career of arguably Arsenal's greatest ever captain. Adams recounts an anecdote in his autobiography about his debut for the Gunners as a 16-year-old. He explains that 'Kenny... did his best to loosen me up in the dressing room,' adding that Sansom had told him: 'Don't worry. If the ball comes to you, you know what to do, don't you? Yes, that's right. Panic.'

Adams would ultimately succeed Kenny as captain, taking over during 1987/88. The season had started well for Kenny too. After Arsenal had managed only one point from their opening three games against Liverpool, Manchester United and West Brom, they went on a 12-match unbeaten run which included ten straight wins and Sansom's first goal for three years, the winner against West Ham at Highbury on his 30th birthday.

However, a niggling injury and the arrival of Nigel Winterburn conspired to end Kenny's Highbury career. He would move on to Newcastle in 1988, although his influence would be strongly felt at Arsenal for many years to come. His role in nurturing the emergent Tony Adams would be vital to Arsenal's successes of recent years, as would the example he set to his eventual replacement, Winterburn. 'He was only here for half a season when I came,' recalls Nigel. 'But during those months I watched him and not the game to see what he did and I think I learned enough!'

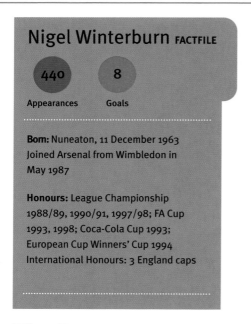

Nigel Winterburn FACTFILE

440 Appearances

8 Goals

Born: Nuneaton, 11 December 1963
Joined Arsenal from Wimbledon in
May 1987

Honours: League Championship
1988/89, 1990/91, 1997/98; FA Cup
1993, 1998; Coca-Cola Cup 1993;
European Cup Winners' Cup 1994
International Honours: 3 England caps

> ' Nigel set an incredible standard from day one... it was a standard he managed to maintain for years. '
>
> Brian Marwood

The Runner-up

Like many of George Graham's early signings, Nigel Winterburn was a player with a determined spirit that was not easily dimmed. He was also a player of considerable skill and intelligence. It was a formidable cocktail but one which had gone unnoticed by other top-flight managers. Graham, however, had recognized Winterburn's qualities and his foresight was rewarded when the erstwhile Wimbledon defender made the transition to Highbury with considerable ease. Nigel, it seemed, was equally at home with the stars of Arsenal as he had been at Plough Lane.

In his first season as a Gunner, Winterburn had to be patient. Kenny Sansom remained the Club's first-choice number three, so the new boy was forced to fill in at right back while watching the master from close quarters. However, when Sansom moved on to Newcastle in the summer of 1988, Nigel began 13 years as Arsenal's undisputed first-choice left back. The fact that he was capped only three times by his country is still viewed with incomprehension by the Highbury faithful, although a sizeable haul of domestic trophies, which includes three League Championship successes, provides some compensation.

Few pundits would begrudge Nigel his successes, and it would be difficult to find a player who has worked with more dedication to achieve his goals. Of course, his first goal was simply to win a place in the Arsenal line-up and prove himself a worthy successor to the likes of Sansom, Sammy Nelson and Bob McNab in the Arsenal defence. It was a task he took to with gusto and no shortage of application.

Winterburn's consistency and supreme professionalism would probably not have come as any great surprise to George Graham, who would have noted that Nigel had been chosen as Wimbledon's player of the year in each of the four seasons he spent at Plough Lane. In the years that followed, Winterburn went on to join David O'Leary, Tony Adams and George Armstrong as one of the top four Arsenal players in terms of appearances, winning seven major honours in the process.

Former team-mate Brian Marwood describes Nigel as 'one hell of a consistent player and one of the most reliable full backs around'. He adds: 'He was quite quiet in the dressing room but I got on well with him, both as a person and as a team-mate with whom I would have to work closely down the left-hand side. He certainly made a great job of replacing one of England's greatest ever left backs in Kenny Sansom.

'Nigel set an incredible standard from day one, but it was a standard he managed to maintain for years. It was a shame that he had Stuart Pearce in his way at international level, because he certainly deserved greater England recognition than he got. Like Lee Dixon, Nigel worked hard on the training ground to improve his game and at Club level at least he got his rewards. I was lucky enough to play in front of Nigel when he eventually took over from Kenny and he was such a good player to have backing me up. He would constantly give me the ball and encourage me to take on the full back, while supporting me from behind.'

Winterburn's contribution, like that of all the Arsenal back four, to the Club's success was immeasurable. His first season at Highbury had ended in disappointment with a penalty miss in the League Cup final defeat by Luton, but from then on it was success all the way for one of the most honest, hard-working professionals in the game. Nigel was one of only three ever-presents in the Championship-winning side of 1988/89 (David Rocastle and keeper John Lukic being the other two) and two of the three goals he scored that season came during the run-in, including a cherished one against his old club Wimbledon, in a 2–2 draw which meant the title race went to the last game at Anfield.

Going about his business with the least possible fuss, but with maximum effort, Nigel became a firm fans' favourite; not least for his solo celebrations of almost every Arsenal goal. These usually involved jumping and running along the touchlines in front of the stands to the delight of supporters who labelled him 'Nutty Boy' as a result.

The ovation he was given when he came off after his final home game for the Club against Sheffield Wednesday in May 2000, spoke volumes about the esteem in which he is held, not least by Arsène Wenger. On Nigel's departure to West Ham, Wenger said: 'He is a special character and I have to say that I and undoubtedly the supporters, did not want him to leave.'

Bergkamp celebrates a rare Winterburn goal.

The Contenders

Ashley Cole, 1999–present
(78 appearances, 6 goals)

At the start of the 2000/01 season Ashley Cole had just one Arsenal first-team appearance under his belt and was sent out on loan to Crystal Palace for three months to gain experience. By the end of that campaign he was Arsenal's first-choice left back, he had played in the Champions League and been called up to represent his country, all at the age of 19.

A product of the Arsenal Academy, initially as a striker, Cole returned to Highbury from Selhurst Park to generous praise, and with an ambition to make the number three shirt his own. When called upon to replace Silvinho in January 2001, it was clear that he had reaped the benefits of his impressive spell in the Palace first team and he kept his place in the Arsenal side for the remainder of the season, setting remarkably high standards for one so young – notably against Bayern Munich and Valencia as Arsenal reached the quarter-finals of the Champions League.

Sven-Goran Eriksson had seen enough of Cole's class, poise and control to call him into his first England squad in February 2001 before awarding him his international debut in the World Cup qualifier against Albania a month later, opting for the youngster's endeavour ahead of Chris Powell's experience. Cole seized his opportunity, making the left back position his own virtually all the way through to the World Cup finals where he started each of England's games up to the quarter-final defeat by Brazil.

Cole has continued to develop into one of the best attacking full backs in the Premiership and he was a key member of the 'double'-winning team of 2001/02. Already well into double figures in terms of England appearances Ashley is set to become England's most exciting left back since a certain Kenny Sansom.

An acrobatic Ashley Cole keeps the ball in play, 2002/03.

Sammy Nelson on another burst from left back.

Sammy Nelson, 1969–1981
(338 appearances, 12 goals)

Irishman Nelson joined Arsenal as a left winger in 1966 but made no senior appearances for more than three years, instead playing over 100 games for the reserves. It was only in the 1976/77 season that he was able to establish himself as a first-team regular as left back, a role he filled for his country too, playing for Ireland on more than 50 occasions.

As well known for his jaunty, overlapping runs down the flank as he was for his wicked sense of humour, Sammy always wanted to entertain. He played the game with a smile but always with 100 per cent commitment. He could be full-blooded in the tackle and was always brave and consistently wholehearted.

Nelson made 338 first-team appearances for Arsenal before departing for Brighton in 1981, his total number of games for the Club at all levels amounting to well over 750. He was an FA Cup finalist three years running, between 1978 and 1980, but the triumph in 1979 represented his only winners' medal.

Bob McNab, 1966–1975
(366 appearances, 6 goals)

Unlike Sammy Nelson, who ultimately succeeded him at left back, Bob wasn't renowned for his attacking prowess. According to former keeper Bob Wilson, however: 'If you are talking purely about defenders, he was better than anybody I've seen. Attacking wise he wasn't the greatest, but the first job of a defender is to defend.'

McNab joined Arsenal in the autumn of 1966, having turned down the opportunity to team up with Bill Shankly at Liverpool, and quickly established himself before playing a vital part in the Club's Fairs Cup success in 1970 and the League Championship and FA Cup success of 1971 – making 62 appearances in total during that season. He also won four England caps between 1968 and 1969 although many people would say it should have been more.

A crisp tackler who was both disciplined and organized, McNab was often the loudest member of the back four and could be heard barking out instructions to his team-mates, notably when the offside trap was being pressed into operation. An intelligent and thoughtful player, he left the Club in 1975 and had a brief spell with Wolves before joining the 'soccer' revolution in the United States where he later coached, being credited with the discovery of such talent as Preki and Paolo Wanchope.

Always focused, Bob McNab was a born leader.

Patrick Vieira FACTFILE

218 Appearances

19 Goals

Born: Dakar, Senegal, 23 June 1976
Joined Arsenal from AC Milan on
14 August 1996

Honours: League Championship
1997/98, 2001/02; FA Cup 1998, 2002
International Honours: 62 France caps;
World Cup 1998; European
Championship 2000

'Vieira is my captain and he takes the **role** very **seriously** and has the respect of everybody.'

Arsène Wenger

It is hard to talk about Patrick Vieira without resorting to cliché and hyperbole. The Senegalese-born France international is – we are told – the 'perfect modern footballer', an 'immense figure', a 'vital presence' and the 'heartbeat' of Wenger's Arsenal. At the time of writing, he has been at Highbury for seven seasons and his achievements speak for themselves. Twice a 'double' winner and with a host of personal awards to his credit, Patrick is one of those rare players who has the talent and application to sustain peak levels of performance and, with them, continued success.

The 6ft 4in Vieira arrived at Arsenal from AC Milan in 1996, and his signing was announced at the same time as that of Remi Garde. Garde was an experienced player who had already won international caps for France, while Patrick was only 20 years old and was said to be a promising midfielder who had endured a difficult one-season sojourn in Milan following a transfer from French club Cannes.

However, despite his youth and his troubled time in Milan, Patrick was an instant hit at Highbury. He made his home debut as a substitute for David Platt in a 4–1 win against Sheffield Wednesday in September 1996, and at season's end he had clocked up an impressive total of 31 Premiership appearances – more than any other Arsenal midfielder that season. His commitment was obvious and his wholehearted performances were met with rapturous approval from the stands, while his selfless team play and considerable skill were greatly appreciated by his team-mates.

Patrick has grown in stature with every passing season as an Arsenal player, not only as a midfielder but also as a leader. If ever there was a natural successor

> Playing for Arsenal has made this guy a better player and a better man. Quickly his opinion counted – because the other players listened to him.
>
> Tony Adams

Patrick has eyes only for the ball, 1997/98.

> He's possibly the best midfielder in the world right now, certainly the best defensive midfielder in the world.

Thierry Henry

to Tony Adams, it is Vieira, and the most successful captain in Arsenal's history agrees that Patrick was the perfect choice to follow him when he retired in 2002: 'Patrick never played like a foreign player and, for me, he was the perfect successor. I knew that the moment he arrived. There was something about him – a presence. At the start he was helped by the fact that the coach was a Frenchman, and Remi Garde was here too.

'Patrick quickly became imbued with English culture – on and off the pitch. Playing for Arsenal has made this guy a better player and a better man. Quickly his opinion counted – because the other players listened to him. Today he is the symbol of English football. It was a great moment for me to become Arsenal skipper, one of the greatest of my career – and I know Patrick felt the same way.'

Not only did Vieira become 'imbued' with English culture, as Adams described it, he also made it part of his duty as an Arsenal player to learn as much as he could about the history of the Club, its great players, its great moments. Former Arsenal midfielder Paul Davis, who is now an Academy coach at the club, remembers wondering if Patrick was aware of who he was and what he had achieved during his own Highbury career. 'I'd seen him around and would nod to him at the training ground but I wasn't sure what he knew about me. I thought he might just presume I was helping out with the coaching,' explains Paul. 'But then I met him at a function and had the opportunity to chat with him so I asked him if he knew who I was. Patrick looked almost insulted by the question, and he instantly said, "Of course I know who you are!" and then he went on to tell me how long I'd been at the Club, what I'd won, etc, etc. It just went to prove that he has a genuine affection for Arsenal Football Club and a great understanding of the Club's history.'

It is little wonder that Vieira has such an affinity with the Arsenal fans, especially since taking over the role of captain from Adams. It is a mantle he has continued to carry with great distinction and manager Arsène Wenger says: 'Patrick is following Tony Adams as a leader and has learned a lot from him. He grows game by game, and the whole team stands behind him. There are many leaders in the team who stand up and take responsibility, but Vieira is my captain and he takes the role very seriously and has the respect of everybody.'

However, Patrick already had the respect of his team-mates long before he wore the captain's armband. His inspirational qualities had also long been obvious, and they were never more clearly demonstrated than against Tottenham Hotspur in the FA Cup semi-final of 2001. It was a match in which Arsenal fell behind early on and spent much of the first half struggling to turn territorial domination into goals. On 33 minutes Patrick took responsibility in emphatic style, picking up the ball in midfield and surging forward to score an equaliser. It was an exemplary act that inspired his team-mates and terrified his opponents. Patrick never relinquished his hold on the game and Arsenal won 2–1. There are many other examples of the Frenchman's ability to dictate vital games... the 3–2 win against Manchester United in November 1998 and the FA Cup final win against Chelsea in 2002 are two that immediately spring to mind.

Thierry Henry is in no doubt as to the quality of his compatriot, whom he describes as 'the best in the world'. Henry explains: 'Patrick has incredible power and mental strength and it is almost unbelievable what he does. He may have felt that some people doubted whether he was the right person to be Arsenal skipper but we had no doubts.

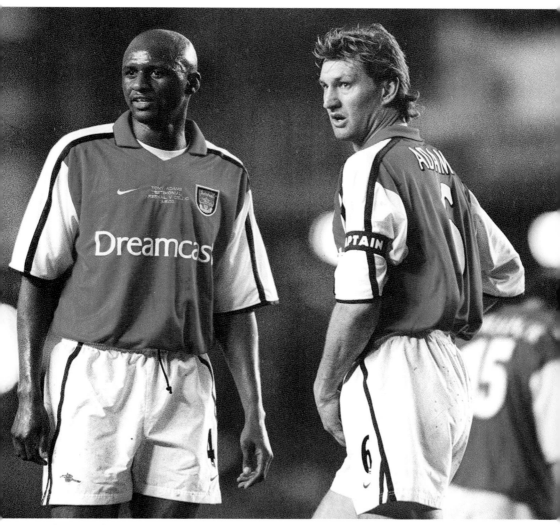

Leaders together: Patrick Vieira and Tony Adams stand side by side, 2001/02.

I want to make my mark in the history of the Club, to be one of its great players, a legend.

Patrick Vieira

'He's already a legend at the Club and, in every game he plays, he writes another page of that storybook. I'm proud to be playing alongside him. He's possibly the best midfielder in the world right now, certainly the best defensive midfielder in the world.'

Vieira himself believes that the additional responsibility of the Highbury captaincy helped him take his game to a higher level. However, he admits he was somewhat taken aback when he was invited to fill the void left by Adams's departure and 'didn't know what to think' when Wenger bestowed the honour upon him. Although he was already a European and world champion, he wasn't sure what the reaction of his Arsenal team-mates would be and he recalls: 'I told the boss that I wanted to talk to a few players about it. They gave me their blessing so I accepted it. The captaincy has made me improve and given me more responsibility. It has made me feel more responsible on the pitch.'

It is impossible to over-estimate the importance of Patrick to Arsenal's recent successes. He embodies everything that Arsène Wenger's team are about – and never more so than during the 2001/02 'double'-winning season when he was so often the driving force for Wenger's team. Patrick's immense contribution was unquestionable and how rewarding it must be for Arsène Wenger that his first Arsenal signing has become such an important figure.

The final word comes from Patrick. When asked what, ultimately, he wanted to achieve as an Arsenal player, he replied: 'I want to make my mark in the history of the Club, to be one of its great players, a legend.' Few would disagree that he has achieved such status already.

Left: Captain Vieira celebrates with Sol Campbell and Ashley Cole after their 2001/02 League-winning performance at Old Trafford.

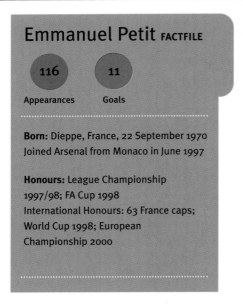

Emmanuel Petit FACTFILE

116 Appearances

11 Goals

Born: Dieppe, France, 22 September 1970
Joined Arsenal from Monaco in June 1997

Honours: League Championship
1997/98; FA Cup 1998
International Honours: 63 France caps;
World Cup 1998; European
Championship 2000

' Manu's long passing was second to none... they [Vieira and Petit] seemed to have a telepathy between them. '

Nigel Winterburn on Emmanuel Petit's contribution to the 1997/98 'double'.

The Runner-up

Few players have achieved more at one club in such a short space of time as Emmanuel Petit did during his three seasons as a Gunner in the late 1990s. The powerfully built Frenchman arrived at Highbury as a utility player who had spent most of his career as a defender. He departed London N5 at the end of the 1999/2000 season with a reputation as a world-class midfielder and with a haul of trophies that included the World Cup, the Premiership title and the FA Cup.

Arsène Wenger had coached Emmanuel at Monaco and was clearly aware that his qualities extended beyond the realm of 'utility man'. Wenger saw his new signing as a midfielder, playing alongside Patrick Vieira in the Arsenal engine room. It was a combination that was somewhat revolutionary in English football. Both players were energetic, powerful and committed. Both were tenacious, strong in the tackle and dogged in their desire to win the ball. It was not the typical combination of ball-winner and playmaker that was the staple fare of the Premiership. However, what many people failed to appreciate was that Emmanuel and Patrick were both constructive players with the ability to play a telling pass or beat an opponent with some fleet footwork.

Emmanuel quickly adapted to the demands of his new role, new club and the new environment of English football. By Christmas he was earning rave reviews, with pundits applauding his ability to dominate games with a blend of energy and enterprise that was matched only by his colleague Vieira. It was incredible to see these two midfield giants in tandem and their partnership was the driving force behind Arsenal's surge towards the Premiership and FA Cup 'double'.

By the time Emmanuel scored his first goal for the Gunners in a 5–0 win against Wimbledon in April 1998 he was already a firm favourite with the Highbury crowd. His goal against the Dons was rapturously celebrated by supporters who had taken the pony-tailed midfielder to their hearts. A month later, he was being fêted for his contribution to the FA Cup final victory over Newcastle United at Wembley, when his delicately floated pass led to Marc Overmars's opening goal in a 2–0 win.

Emmanuel's first season at Highbury ended with the 'double'. He had missed only eight League and Cup games all season and had contributed two goals and many more assists.

It was a record that earned him a place in Aimé Jacquet's World Cup squad for France '98, and an already unforgettable season was capped when the Arsenal midfielder galloped on to Patrick Vieira's pass to score France's third goal in the final against Brazil.

After such achievements, Petit and Vieira both found that their profiles had been significantly raised by the successes of 1998. Rumour and speculation would follow them henceforward. They would also become both the template and target for Premiership midfielders. Other managers were desperate to unearth similar talents, and it was no surprise to see the likes of Olivier Dacourt, the late Marc-Vivien Foé and Didier Deschamps arrive in English football soon afterwards. Meanwhile, there was a growing sense that teams had realized that to stop Arsenal from playing they would have to stop Petit and Vieira. All tried but few succeeded.

Emmanuel suffered with a number of minor injuries during his remaining two seasons with the Club. However, when fit, his contributions were still considerable. He scored four times in 26 League appearances in 1998/99, following up with three goals in 26 matches during his final campaign. He also played in all but one of Arsenal's nine UEFA Cup fixtures, making his last appearance in a Gunners jersey in the competition's final against Galatasaray in Copenhagen.

In the summer of 2000, Petit helped France add the European Championship crown to the World Cup trophy won on home soil two years earlier. It was a considerable achievement for a footballer who had been no more than a fringe player for Les Bleus prior to his move to Highbury in 1997. He was by then much coveted by Europe's biggest clubs, and shortly after Euro 2000 he moved to Barcelona.

Despite the move to the Nou Camp and a later transfer to Chelsea, Petit still has great affection for Arsenal and especially for Wenger, whom he describes as 'the greatest man I know'.

Manu celebrates his first Arsenal goal, against Wimbledon in 1998.

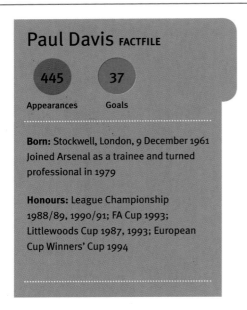

Paul Davis FACTFILE

445
Appearances

37
Goals

Born: Stockwell, London, 9 December 1961
Joined Arsenal as a trainee and turned
professional in 1979

Honours: League Championship
1988/89, 1990/91; FA Cup 1993;
Littlewoods Cup 1987, 1993; European
Cup Winners' Cup 1994

Third Place

Like Liam Brady, Arsenal's midfield master at the time he made his first-team breakthrough in 1980, Paul was an educated midfielder with an excellent range of passes. During his 16-year career at Highbury, Paul made 445 League appearances, scoring 37 goals, and his trophy haul would grace the cabinet of many of the greatest English players.

Two League Championship winners' medals, from 1988/89 and 1990/91, take pride of place in his collection of honours, but probably the 1994 triumph over Parma in the European Cup Winners' Cup final holds the greatest affection for a player who had been used sparingly in the League by George Graham, but who was an ever-present throughout that European campaign.

Because he was under-used in the quest for the League Championship, Paul began to consider a future away from Highbury. He recalls that 'there was a time when I did ask George Graham for a transfer', but his Cup Winners' Cup involvement eased the disappointment and he remembers the night of the final well.

'We weren't really given a chance, we had injuries and suspensions and we were facing a

team which had the likes of Brolin, Asprilla and Zola, all of whom were in their prime,' he recollects. 'To come through that and win that game showed the spirit that we had. I'd been out of the side for a while and it was a good opportunity for me to show what I could do. I enjoyed that competition.'

A year later Paul did indeed leave Arsenal, on a free transfer. Former team-mate Viv Anderson believes his contribution sometimes went unnoticed: 'Paul was a wonderful footballer with a cultured left foot, a lot like Graham Rix who shared the left-sided duties, but for some reason he was very under-rated; he deserves immense credit for giving Arsenal Football Club 16 years of great service.'

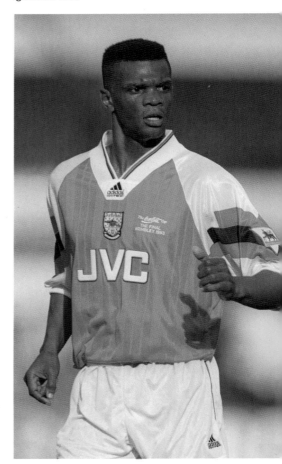

Paul Davis... a loyal Arsenal servant.

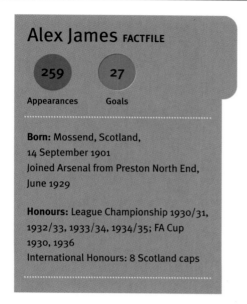

Alex James FACTFILE

259
Appearances

27
Goals

Born: Mossend, Scotland,
14 September 1901
Joined Arsenal from Preston North End,
June 1929

Honours: League Championship 1930/31,
1932/33, 1933/34, 1934/35; FA Cup
1930, 1936
International Honours: 8 Scotland caps

Fourth Place

Alex James was arguably the single most important player in the great Arsenal teams of the 1930s. James was the man who linked defence and attack, distributing a seemingly endless supply of passes to wingers Cliff Bastin and Joe Hulme, and setting up a succession of goals for his fellow team-mates. With his confident swagger and trademark baggy shorts, Alex was an instantly recognizable figure, and it is significant that Arsenal had won nothing prior to his arrival but were soon sweeping all before them in both the League and Cup.

Many of Herbert Chapman's signings in the 1920s and 1930s were unproven players of, as yet, unfulfilled promise. Men like Cliff Bastin, Herbie Roberts and Eddie Hapgood had no profile in the game prior to joining Arsenal. Alex James, however, was already a household name when he sauntered in to London, N5. He had been Preston North End's star player, scoring 60 goals in little over 150 appearances, and he had also been Man of the Match and a double goalscorer for Scotland's Wembley Wizards who conquered England so convincingly in 1928.

Unsurprisingly, when Preston made Alex available for transfer in the summer of 1929, all the big clubs were interested but – not for the first time – Arsenal manager Herbert Chapman got his man, seeing off interest from the likes of Aston Villa and Liverpool.

However, while most observers had been impressed by Alex's marauding inside-forward play and goalscoring potency, Chapman had been focussing on the Scotsman's technique and vision. The Arsenal manager had recognized a player who could fill the vital role at the hub of his new third-back formation. Chapman did not need Alex to join attacks, he needed him to instigate them, and his raking passing from the middle of the field soon became famous.

James adapted to the new role with ease, and where previously he had been free to attack with gusto, he now began to play with greater discipline. James's goalscoring record inevitably suffered, although he remained a capable finisher, as he proved in the 1930 FA Cup final against Huddersfield, when he scored the opening goal after a neat interchange of passes with Bastin.

Bastin once commented: 'Nobody has greater faith in the qualities of Alex James than Alex James himself – not even Herbert Chapman, and that is saying something.' It was undoubtedly true that Chapman regarded James – who he made his captain – as Arsenal's star player. The manager would allow James certain extra privileges, for example, he was allowed to stay in bed longer than the other players on match days, but it did not appear to affect morale and James remained a popular figure with his team-mates.

By the time Arsenal won the FA Cup for the second time in 1936, Alex James was 34. His performances had not yet dimmed – in fact, he had scored his only Arsenal hat-trick against Sheffield Wednesday just a year earlier – but after one more season the Scotsman decided the time was right to hang up his boots. Alex played his final game for Arsenal against Feyenoord during a summer tour match in 1937. He would take a job with a pools firm shortly afterwards but would return to Highbury as a coach after the Second World War. However, in 1953, Alex died at the age of just 51.

Frank McLintock FACTFILE

403 Appearances

32 Goals

Born: Glasgow, 28 December 1939
Joined Arsenal from Leicester City in
October 1964

Honours: League Championship 1970/71;
FA Cup 1971; European Fairs Cup 1970
International Honours: 9 Scotland caps

'Although not the biggest, Frank was a good enough size

and his **heart** was **bigger**

than anyone's.'

Alan Ball

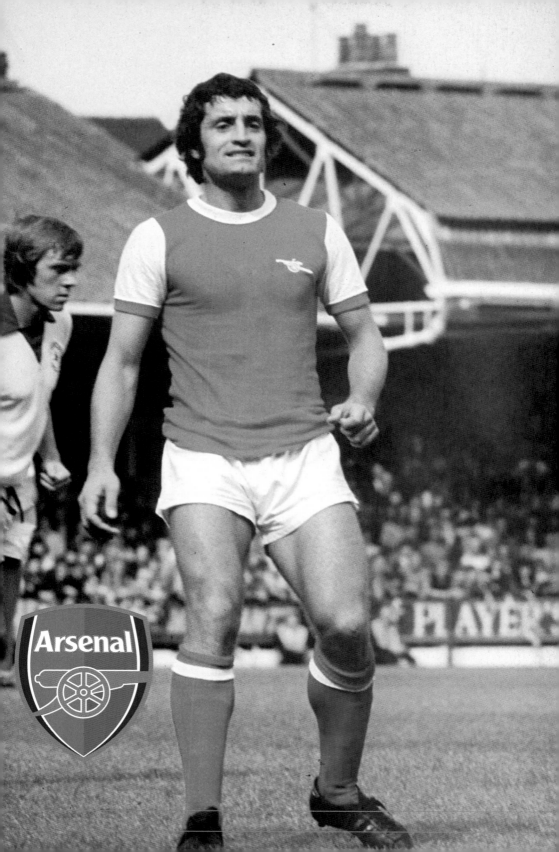

Impulsive, effervescent and always committed, Frank McLintock was the inspirational captain of Bertie Mee's 'double'-winning team of 1970/71. As a footballer Frank was undeniably talented but it was his leadership skills rather than his ball skills that set the affable Scot apart from his rivals. One former colleague, Bob Wilson, put it succinctly: 'As a centre half Frank was less than perfect but as a leader he was absolutely exceptional.'

Although a Glaswegian brought up in the city's tough Gorbals district, Frank began his professional career in England with Leicester City. He arrived at Filbert Street as an 18-year-old wing half and remained a midfielder throughout his time with the Foxes, helping them reach two FA Cup finals – both of which they lost – in 1961 and 1963.

Billy Wright was clearly impressed by the midfield performances of the young McLintock, and in October 1964 he brought the 24-year-old Scot to Highbury. Frank arrived to join a team that was low on confidence and consistency but high on big-name stars. Joe Baker, George Eastham and Don Howe were among Wright's first-team squad but despite their presence, Arsenal were struggling in the League and making little headway in Cup competitions.

Frank brought much-needed energy to the Arsenal midfield. He not only had great stamina but also incomparable levels of commitment. Bob Wilson recalls, 'Frank has an impulsive nature, which was something that also helped him become a great captain. When he played in midfield he would sometimes let his heart rule his head though, and, if we were losing, he'd end up charging all over the place.'

However, it would be wrong to portray Frank as merely a midfield workhorse. He was a player of considerable skill, too, and possessed all the technique needed to become a top-class attacking midfielder. His stamina was prodigious, his control effortless and his passing both accurate and economical; add to that

> As a leader he was absolutely exceptional.
>
> Bob Wilson

Frank was a constructive player who would carry the ball forward from the back.

an eye for goal and excellent heading ability, and you have a footballer of considerable talent.

For five years Frank was a stalwart in Arsenal's midfield, during which time the Club reached two Cup finals. Both ended in defeat, first with Leeds, in 1968, and then Swindon Town a year later overcoming them in the League Cup. For Frank it meant four successive defeats in finals and the unwanted tag of 'jinx'. However, his career was on the verge of a major change as the 1960s drew to a close.

An injury crisis in the 1969/70 season left Arsenal with problems in defence and, as had so often been the case, Don Howe found an inspired solution. Howe asked Frank to move back to centre half and, after initial reticence, he agreed. It looked like a gamble on Howe's part. Frank was neither the tallest of players – 5ft 10in was a modest height for a centre half in an era of battering-ram strikers – nor was he noted for his tactical discipline. But the Arsenal coach had clearly seen something to make him believe that Frank could make a go of things at the heart of defence.

There was inevitably a period of adjustment, but he soon began to look assured and comfortable at centre half. 'Once he was put into the back four and he'd grown into the position his game improved,' says Wilson. 'His passion and his preparedness to get hurt were perhaps his greatest attributes as a player. He was also very fortunate that alongside him he had one of the steadiest and most consistent footballers I ever played with in Peter Simpson. Peter was solid.'

Alan Ball has a similar view of his former Arsenal team-mate: 'Although not the biggest, Frank was a good enough size and his heart was bigger than anyone's.'

The combination of the steady and reliable Simpson with the more instinctive and aggressive McLintock was close to perfection. It was also a partnership that did much to end two trophyless decades for Arsenal, with both players starring in the European Fairs Cup victory of 1969/70. Frank was by now Club captain and when his team lost the first leg of the Fairs Cup final to Anderlecht in Belgium, he was distraught. 'We lost 3–1 with Ray Kennedy scoring in the dying minutes to give us a lifeline,' recalls Bob Wilson, who was in goal that night. 'But when we got in the dressing room Frank was the most upset player in there initially. However, by the time we left the dressing room he was the one who was saying, "We'll stuff this lot when we get them back to Highbury." And, sure enough, we did.'

Reflecting once more on McLintock's 'impulsiveness', Wilson emphasizes that it 'could work to his advantage. He was an extraordinary captain. He'd be right in your face if he thought you'd done something wrong.'

 Frank was an inspirational leader, second to none. He commanded respect by the way he played and treated people on and off the field.
Charlie George

Frank's leadership qualities would be put to full use during the 1970/71 'double' season. He missed only one of Arsenal's 64 games that season and was ever-present in both the League and FA Cup. His penchant for attacking also saw him contribute five goals en route to the Championship, including a run of three in five important games during April. However, it was Frank's stoic defensive performance against Spurs in the final League match of the season that will live longest in the memory. If Arsenal kept a clean sheet against their local rivals, they would be champions, but if they conceded a goal, a draw would no longer be good enough. It was imperative that Frank and his defensive colleagues shut out Spurs, but that would not be easy in a tense local derby, particularly when the Spurs line-up included the likes of Chivers, Gilzean and Martin Peters.

Arsenal fans mob Frank after the Gunners clinch the 1970/71 Championship.

Frank holds aloft the FA Cup at Wembley in 1971.

Frank proved himself up to the task, shadowing Martin Chivers with diligence and authority, while simultaneously cajoling and encouraging his team-mates. At the end of the game, the Arsenal skipper was rightly chaired off the pitch. The celebrations would go on long into the night at the White Hart in Southgate, as Frank and his colleagues toasted the League Championship. However, five days later the team had an appointment at Wembley to contest the second leg of the 'double'.

For Frank it was a fifth Cup final appearance at Wembley, and the Scot was eager to improve on his record of four defeats. The match against Liverpool proved a cagey affair and it was not until extra time that the Arsenal defence was breached by Steve Heighway's shot. An equalizer from Eddie Kelly followed, but it was left to Charlie George to add the legendary goal from 20 yards for the 2–1 victory. Nobody was more delighted than McLintock by Charlie's goal, and after the game he was so eager to collect the trophy that Bob Wilson implored him to slow down and savour the moment.

George was the undoubted hero of the 1971 Cup final, but he is quick to pay tribute to the contribution of his captain throughout a famous season. 'Frank was an inspirational leader, second to none. He commanded respect by the way he played and treated people on and off the field. I don't think anyone has got more out of his players than Frank. Always there, always encouraging, and cajoling when necessary, he got the last drop of blood out of every Arsenal player who wore the shirt beside him.'

Frank's performances during the 'double' season earned him the Footballer of the Year award in 1971, a accolade which was followed by an MBE a year later.

Alas, there would be no more silverware for the Arsenal captain, who found himself once more a Wembley loser in 1972 when Leeds emerged victorious after a 1–0 win in the FA Cup final. Within a year, he had been sold to Queens Park Rangers. Mee had decided he needed to rebuild his team and it was time for McLintock – like George Graham and Charlie George – to move on.

At 33, however, Frank remained a fit and willing competitor, continuing to give his all. They were qualities demonstrated by McLintock's contribution to a Queens Park Rangers side that narrowly missed out on the Championship in 1975/76.

Frank went on to sample management with first Leicester City and later Brentford, but it is as a media pundit that he is now most familiar. And Frank McLintock the pundit, much like Frank McLintock the player, is always honest and frequently impassioned.

David O'Leary FACTFILE

722 Appearances

14 Goals

Born: Stoke Newington, London
2 May 1958
Joined Arsenal as an apprentice in July 1973

Honours: League Championship
1988/89, 1990/91; FA Cup 1979, 1993;
Littlewoods Cup 1987, Coca-Cola Cup 1993
International Honours: 68 Republic
of Ireland caps

6 He was more of a European style player than British, never looked aggressive but got the job done. 9

Charlie Nicholas

The Runner-up

As a player David O'Leary appeared calm and laid back but as a manager the softly spoken Irishman revealed the passionate and at times ambitious streak that had driven him throughout a record-breaking 20-year Arsenal career. No player has played more first-team games for Arsenal, while his collection of trophies includes a complete set of major domestic honours.

Although born in Stoke Newington, David was raised in Dublin – hence the unmistakable brogue – and began his junior football career with Shelbourne. However, as captain of the Republic of Ireland schoolboy team, there was little chance that he would remain undetected by scouts from England. Arsenal, of course, were the team who clinched David's signature, and in 1973 the 15-year-old O'Leary began his apprenticeship at Highbury along with compatriots Liam Brady and Frank Stapleton.

The coincidence of these three talented Irishmen in the Highbury youth ranks was extremely welcome to the side of the mid-1970s, but while all of them made a rapid ascent to the first team, they would later take radically different career paths. Both Brady and Stapleton departed

the Club while in their prime; O'Leary, however, remained loyal for two decades. The fact that David stayed, when surely there must have been other interested parties, was not lost on the fans, who took him to their hearts.

The Highbury crowd had their first taste of the teenage O'Leary during the 1975/76 season and were quickly impressed. Bertie Mee and Don Howe had been similarly impressed after watching the lightly built teenager give a succession of masterful displays against John Radford and Ray Kennedy in practice matches. 'I used to play against this kid in training,' recalls Radford. 'He didn't give me a kick. I used to get really mad. He was tall so he had no problem in the air, his pace was deceptive – ever so quick – and he tackled well. David was comfortable on the ball as well.'

By the age of 21, David was an FA Cup winner and a fixture in Terry Neill's team, although his calm and mature displays belied his youth. His composure, both as a defender and when in possession of the ball, was exemplary, as was his reading of the game, and he did everything possible to avoid last-ditch tackles. Instead, he would intercept when others might stand off, and he would always look to jockey opponents away from the danger zone rather than dive in.

Of course, when required to make a dramatic dash, David revealed a deceptive turn of pace.

Former team-mate Chris Whyte describes him as 'Quick... he could always get himself out of trouble and his overall game was reliable. David usually avoided conflict by speed of thought. He anticipated the play and nipped in to snuff out the danger before it developed.'

David gave arguably his best performance in an Arsenal shirt on a night that ended in misery after a penalty shoot-out defeat against Valencia in the 1980 European Cup Winners' Cup final. Up against World Cup-winning Argentinian striker Mario Kempes, the young Irishman gave a masterclass in the art of defending, marking his illustrious opponent with calm authority.

In the mid-1980s David enjoyed a spell as Club captain, but the armband had passed to Tony Adams by the time success returned to Highbury under George Graham. Nevertheless, the experienced Eire international remained an important figure during the League Cup success of 1987. David would also reveal his versatility during the 1988/89 Championship season, playing in a variety of roles including right back and sweeper.

David had made his debut for the Republic of Ireland as an 18-year-old under John Giles, but the highlight of an impressive 68-cap international career probably came during the 1990 World Cup in Italy. David demonstrated a hitherto unseen talent when he scored the deciding penalty in a second-phase shoot-out against Romania.

At club level David continued to taste glory. Once more he was a willing and versatile contributor to a Championship success, making 21 appearances in 1990/91. He added to his haul of silverware by coming on as a substitute in the 1993 FA Cup final win over Sheffield Wednesday, but the same match also brought the conclusion to his Highbury career. After 17 seasons in the first team and five major honours, David O'Leary moved on for a brief stay at Leeds United. Returning to Elland Road as manager, O'Leary began to display an inner strength and a serious commitment that surprised many who could recall his relaxed appearance on the pitch.

There is, however, no denying David O'Leary's quality as a footballer and as a leader. 'O'Leary was a good communicator but not in the forceful manner of McLintock or Adams,' recalled Charlie Nicholas. 'He was a great passer and showed great calmness on the ball. He was more of a European style player than British, never looked aggressive but got the job done. An intelligent player.' However, as he has shown as a manager, his calm demeanour disguises a steely self-confidence.

David has the ball under control, mid-1970s.

Martin Keown FACTFILE

434
Appearances

4
Goals

Born: Oxford, 24 July 1966
Joined Arsenal as an apprentice in
January 1984. Rejoined from Everton in
February 1993

Honours: League Championship
1997/98, 2001/02; FA Cup 1998,
2002, 2003
International Honours: 43 England caps

Third Place

According to football lore, players should never return to their former clubs. Thankfully, in 1993, Martin Keown chose to ignore superstition and re-signed for Arsenal, having left as a 20-year-old in 1986. It is a decision for which the Club in general and Arsène Wenger in particular have frequently been grateful.

Martin joined Arsenal as an apprentice in 1984 and a year later broke into Don Howe's first team. Even then, he displayed the dogged approach to defending that would soon become his trademark, but he was also regarded as a constructive player, and effective when in possession.

A promising partnership with David O'Leary was halted when Martin joined Aston Villa, while Tony Adams took his place alongside O'Leary at Arsenal. His stay at Villa Park took in both relegation and promotion before he moved to Everton. At Goodison Park Martin's profile grew and in 1992 he earned an England cap against Czechoslovakia, marking his debut with a memorable goal from the edge of the box.

A year later, he took the decision to return to Highbury and compete for a central-defensive place. The early years of his second spell at Arsenal were frustrating; the Cup-tied former Evertonian had to sit out both Cup successes of 1993 and he was injured for the Cup Winners' Cup triumph of 1994. During the rest of George Graham's reign and throughout Bruce Rioch's managership, Martin played in a host of positions. One week he was at left back, the next right back and, for an extended spell under Rioch, he played as a holding midfielder.

It was under Arsène Wenger's tutelage that he was given the chance to show his true quality as a central defender. Playing alongside Tony Adams, Martin became the fifth member of a famous Arsenal defence. His controlled aggression and talent for man-marking was a major factor in the 'double' successes of 1997/98 and 2001/02, and under Glenn Hoddle Martin emerged as an international regular in his early 30s.

In his 37th year, Martin Keown has shown little sign that he is losing motivation. He remained a key figure in Arsène Wenger's team throughout the title defence of 2002/03, prompting Joe Baker to comment: 'Martin Keown has impressed me a lot with his rugged and uncompromising attitude. He is a very good player and doesn't always get the credit he deserves.'

Martin celebrates a goal with the Highbury faithful.

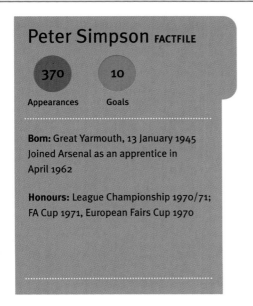

Peter Simpson FACTFILE

370
Appearances

10
Goals

Born: Great Yarmouth, 13 January 1945
Joined Arsenal as an apprentice in
April 1962

Honours: League Championship 1970/71;
FA Cup 1971, European Fairs Cup 1970

> " He was absolutely superb and very unfortunate not to get an England cap. If he was around today he would be a regular in the national side. "
>
> Frank McLintock

Fourth Place

Peter Simpson was a player whose contribution was immense but who rarely took the credit he deserved. The pivotal defender in Bertie Mee's 'double'-winning team of 1970/71, he was the disciplined, steady centre half alongside the maverick Frank McLintock in the heart of Arsenal's defence.

McLintock regards his former defensive partner as a player of the highest calibre. 'He was absolutely superb and very unfortunate not to get an England cap. If he was around today he would be a regular in the national side... a quiet unassuming man off the park but superbly confident on it.'

The Norfolk-born stopper made his Arsenal debut as a 19-year-old against Chelsea in March 1965 but it proved a traumatic occasion as he was left to watch the man he was marking (Bobby Tambling) score four times. Fitful appearances followed, with Peter filling in at fullback and in midfield, but it was not until the appointment of Bertie Mee as manager in 1966 that he found a regular place in the Arsenal first team.

Peter played in the League Cup final defeats against Leeds and Swindon in the late 1960s but

his luck improved as the decade turned. First came success in the Fairs Cup of 1969/70 and then, a year later, Mee's men completed the first League and FA Cup 'double' for ten years.

As a defender, Peter brought a calm authority to the Arsenal backline, while his composed and accurate left-footed passing was frequently the springboard for counter-attacks. 'Peter was a real player, he had a great left foot,' recalls Alan Ball. 'I think he would have won as many England caps as Tony [Adams] had he not been unfortunate enough to be there at the same time that Bobby Moore was around.'

The presence of Moore and Leeds's Norman Hunter in Alf Ramsay's England team undoubtedly prevented Peter from enjoying the international recognition that his talents deserved. Included in the initial panel for the 1970 World Cup finals, he was left out of the final 22.

Peter remained at Highbury while many of his former 'double'-winning colleagues departed in Bertie Mee's mid-1970s team rebuilding. He survived Mee's entire reign before heading off to the United States and a fresh challenge with the New England Teamen in the summer of 1978, having made nearly 500 first-team appearances and won many admirers during his 15 years at Arsenal.

'If ever I wanted to explain to a **young player** just how a centre half should play I would point to Tony.'

Former team-mate Steve Williams

It is hard to imagine a more complete centre half than Tony Adams. For the better part of 20 years he was a colossus at the back for Arsenal Football Club, dominating opposing attackers with a devastating blend of power and authority. Of course, Tony was more than just a defender, he was a leader too, and under his captaincy Arsenal were four times Champions and five times winners in major Cup finals. It is an unrivalled record and one that has earned him a peerless position with Arsenal's fans, most of whom regard him as the Club's greatest post-war player.

Tony made his senior debut against Sunderland in November 1983, just weeks after his 17th birthday. He spent the next few seasons on the fringes of the first team, but Charlie Nicholas remembers that Tony already had a certain air of confidence about him, explaining: '...after only six games and at the age of 17, [he] had you asking "Who is he? This guy's just different class"... simplicity was his game and he basically just did his job... Tony had star affinity.'

The 1986/87 season brought Tony to the attention of a wider audience. He became a regular first team player that season, playing in all 55 first-team matches, including the League Cup final win over Liverpool. His contribution did not go unnoticed and he was named PFA Young Player of the Year and earned a call-up to Bobby Robson's England team too, which crowned a memorable season for the prodigiously talented Arsenal defender.

Tony's career at Arsenal seemed to have no bounds, and in 1987 he was appointed Club captain by George Graham. He had previously captained all of his junior teams, so it was a job he was prepared for and for which he seemed destined. At just 21 he had become the youngest captain in Arsenal's history,

People display leadership qualities in different ways and Tony always wore his heart on his sleeve.

Brian Marwood

Adams returns to the first team after four months on the sidelines through injury.

and he recalls in his autobiography that he was 'comfortable with the position', adding, 'I knew I had a lot to offer. It made sense to me, it was the role for me.' It was also a role he would fulfil for 15 years.

Tony was not only George Graham's captain, he was also the pivotal figure in the new look Arsenal defence that the manager was carefully constructing in the late 1980s. Lee Dixon, Nigel Winterburn and Steve Bould would all arrive at Highbury in quick succession, and George worked tirelessly with his new back four on the training ground. However, when it came to matchday, it was left to Tony to organize and orchestrate matters.

In 1988/89 Tony led Arsenal to their first League title for 18 years. The Arsenal captain maintained performances of a consistently high standard, leading by example throughout a memorable season that climaxed with a dramatic title-clinching 2–0 win at Anfield in May 1989. Nigel Winterburn is in no doubt as to the contribution his skipper made: 'Tony just has something about him that makes you push that little bit harder. Whether it was the way he played or what he said, he just typified the Arsenal spirit. I don't think in '89 we were the best team around but we were the most organized and determined and he was the pivotal figure.'

Former team-mate Brian Marwood, who joined the Club in 1987 and shared the 1989 League title success with Adams, is similarly effusive in his praise of the man he says has had 'a massive impact on Arsenal Football Club'. Marwood says: 'People display leadership qualities in different ways and Tony always wore his heart on his sleeve. I knew of him before I went to Arsenal and I was aware of what it was about him that made people believe he was going to be a great player and a great captain. But it was only after joining Arsenal and working with him that I truly appreciated exactly what they were talking about.

'He would dive into areas and put his foot into tackles where others would fear to tread and, even for someone so young at the time, he was an absolute inspiration to others around him. He had no fear whatsoever. He was also a great character and a great personality and an admirable performer.'

In 1990/91 Tony led the Gunners to another League title, and once more defensive fortitude was to prove the secret of Arsenal's success. Graham's team lost only once in the League and conceded just 18 goals in their 38 games. It was an incredible record and one for which Tony could take much credit. His leadership skills and indomitable spirit were by then widely recognized, but he was also starting to exert more influence over his team's attacking play.

Simplicity was his game and he basically just did his job... Tony had star affinity.

Charlie Nicholas on the young Tony Adams

His constructive qualities were often overlooked, but it was frequently Tony who began passing moves from the back, while his aerial ability made him a formidable threat from set pieces.

In 1993 and 1994 Arsenal were grateful to two Adams's goals that earned the Club a place in two Cup finals. The first came against Tottenham Hotspur in the 1993 FA Cup semi-final, while the second arrived en route to the Cup Winners' Cup final and disposed of Italian side Torino. On both occasions, Arsenal went on to win the competitions, enabling Tony to lift his fourth and fifth trophies as captain.

However, persistent knee and ankle injuries would begin to trouble Tony in the mid-1990s and for much of the remainder of his career he would battle against these ailments. As you would expect, the Arsenal skipper never complained, maintaining staggeringly consistent levels of performance and physical commitment.

The arrival of Arsène Wenger at Highbury in 1996, however, offered Tony a new challenge. Could he adapt to the demands of a new coach with radical new ideas? The answer was an emphatic yes. 'With George I simply lived on my wits and instincts,' explained Tony in his autobiography. 'I found myself with Arsène taking much more notice of his methods. I suppose it had something to do with the age I got to as a player and also with a new awareness I had acquired in my life.'

Kanu is first to congratulate his skipper on a goal celebrated gleefully at Highbury.

What a leader, what a player, what a man.

Pat Rice's tribute to Adams

The appointment of Wenger, allied with Tony's growing experience and maturity, saw Adams's game rise to new heights in the late 1990s. He was still just as committed as ever, still capable of dominating centre forwards with his physical strength, but he was now anticipating danger more, calmly snuffing out threatening attacks with interceptions and astute tackles. With the arrival of a wave of foreign imports into English football, many of whom were attackers, defenders had needed to evolve too, and Tony was keeping one step ahead of his adversaries. Whether he was up against a battering-ram centre forward who liked an aerial tussle or a tricky flyweight Brazilian, it mattered little to the Arsenal skipper.

In 1997/98 Tony emulated the feat of another great Arsenal centre half and captain, Frank McLintock, by leading the Club to its second League and Cup 'double'. Between the end of January and the middle of April, Arsenal did not concede a single Premiership goal as they clawed back a 12-point deficit at the top of the table with a staggering run of good form. Significantly, Tony remained ever-present throughout this sequence. His leadership and unstinting confidence were vital to one of the great comebacks in the history of the English Championship. It was fitting, therefore, that Tony should score the final goal in the title-clinching victory over Everton at Highbury on 3 May. It was a goal that will live long in the memories of all who witnessed it.

In the game's final minute, Steve Bould gained possession and moved forward adventurously. Tony darted forward, latching on to a sublime pass from his central-defensive partner, collected the ball and calmly dispatched an inch-perfect shot past the Everton keeper. It was a goal that was celebrated with immense pride by the Highbury faithful.

Four years later, at the age of 36, Tony made Highbury history by captaining Arsenal to a second 'double'. By then, however, his injuries were becoming more troublesome and Wenger was forced to use his captain sparingly, invariably saving him for vital games. The Arsenal skipper's final competitive game in red and white came at the Millennium Stadium against Chelsea in the FA Cup final. It was an appropriate way to bring down the curtain on a glorious career. Tony was at his impeccable best, marshalling his team-mates with supreme authority against a dangerous Chelsea attack. The game ended in a 2–0 victory, with Tony no doubt taking almost as much pleasure from the clean sheet as from victory.

A few days later the Arsenal fans got the chance to give Tony an emotional Highbury send off, on the occasion of his testimonial match against Celtic. More than 38,000 supporters attended, among them assistant manager Pat Rice, who wrote: 'What a leader, what a player, what a man. Have a great retirement with your family. Thanks for all the memories.'

Wenger was also quick to praise the man who had led his team to two 'doubles', explaining: 'I believe that when I arrived here Tony changed his way of life. If he had not done that his career would be over – with or without my influence – so the biggest part has been played by himself, through the strength of his character.

'If he looks back on that now, back to 1996, he can be proud of what he has achieved in his life – both on the pitch and off it. We all know what he has achieved as a player – the amount of trophies he has won is remarkable and there for all to see – but what he has achieved as a man away from football is very important too.'

Tony celebrates the winning goal in the 1993 FA Cup semi-final against Spurs.

Steve Bould FACTFILE

371 Appearances

8 Goals

Born: Stoke, 16 November 1962
Joined Arsenal from Stoke City in
July 1988

Honours: League Championship
1988/89, 1990/91, 1997/98; FA Cup
1993, 1998; Littlewoods Cup 1993;
European Cup Winners' Cup 1994
International Honours: 2 England caps

> **6** If I was looking for a centre half, he is what I would go for: calm, strong, determined, never loses a header. Rock solid. **9**
>
> Tony Adams gives his assessment of Steve Bould's qualities as a centre half

The Runner-up

Steve Bould more than played his part in the Gunners' remarkable run of success over a ten-year period when, while not the most vaunted of the famed backline, he was certainly a key component within it – as his six-medal haul from over 350 appearances clearly illustrates.

An uncompromising and unfussy defender in the main, the former Stoke stopper added an element of sophistication to his play following the arrival of Arsène Wenger and his elegant through ball which set up Tony Adams's Championship-sealing goal against Everton in 1998 prompted the Arsenal manager to liken him, presumably tongue in cheek, to the great Franz Beckenbauer.

A slight exaggeration, perhaps, but also an example of how Bould had developed as a player since his arrival from the Potteries, following the path of his former Stoke team-mate Lee Dixon, in 1988. Playing in such exalted company, Bould did not always get the recognition he deserved,

making his man-of-the-match award in the 1994 Cup Winners' Cup triumph over Parma an honour to savour – almost as much as the belated England call-up which followed a matter of days later. But while he rarely received, or craved, public attention and adulation, he was a valued member of the team and a worthy winner of three Championship medals before finally departing for Sunderland.

Former colleague Brian Marwood, while crediting George Graham for bringing the renowned Arsenal back four together in the first place, also praises Bould and the others for developing an understanding and a partnership unrivalled anywhere in the English game, arguably throughout Europe. Marwood says: 'The balance George achieved in that department was absolutely spot on and yet it was made up of players, Tony Adams aside, who didn't have a massive pedigree in top-flight terms. Steve Bould and Lee Dixon both came from Stoke while Nigel Winterburn had come from Wimbledon, but

George recognized something in all of them that would make them genuine Arsenal players.

'To bring those sort of players together with a young lad in Adams who, essentially, was still learning his trade, was nothing short of genius and, as we all now know, was to be the bedrock of Arsenal's success over many years. Steve Bould more than played his part in that, as was recognized by everyone at the Club even though others outside Highbury might not have had the same high regard for him as we did.

'Mind you, George did work relentlessly with Steve and the other lads on the training field in his quest to achieve perfection. George had acquired a rough diamond which he constantly buffed and polished until it was the most valuable jewel in his crown.'

Paul Davis is in full agreement, although he believes the midfield also did their fair share of protecting and should take a certain amount of credit for ensuring that Bould, Adams and their colleagues enjoyed such career longevity. Paul explains: 'Whenever I see these guys, Steve, Tony, Nigel and Lee, I always remind them of something that George Graham said years ago. It was around 1990 and we were all in our mid-20s. George said to us, "You midfielders are there to protect the back four. That back four is going to play on until they're all about 37 or 38, whereas all you midfielders will be finished by the time you're 32."'

Graham's prediction proved astute and Steve was in his 37th year when he departed Highbury for Sunderland in the summer of 1999. He had contributed greatly to the Club's greatest back four and to a golden era in the history of Arsenal Football Club.

Steve was a formidable presence in the greatest back four British football has seen in recent years.

Sol Campbell FACTFILE

64
Appearances

4
Goals

Born: Newham, London,
18 September 1974
Joined Arsenal from Tottenham Hotspur
in July 2001

Honours: League Championship
2001/02; FA Cup 2002
International Honours: 53 England caps

Third Place

It may still be early days in the Arsenal career of Sol Campbell, but the powerful Londoner has already shown enough quality in his first few seasons as a Gunner to suggest that he is the latest in a long line of top-class centre backs to grace the red and white jersey. The Highbury crowd expects to see a dominant figure at the heart of the Arsenal defence, having been spoilt by the likes of McLintock, O'Leary, Adams, Bould and Keown, and Sol is continuing the tradition.

Strong in the air, unyielding in the tackle and fast over the ground, he has been blessed with the kind of natural talent that cannot be acquired by hard work. Of course, his strength and athleticism has been honed by a widely admired level of professionalism and prodigious efforts on the training ground. It was this combination of attributes that saw Sol become one of football's most coveted players when his contract with Tottenham Hotspur ran out in the summer of 2001.

Sol's decision to follow the path across North London trodden by Willie Young and Pat Jennings in the 1970s was, inevitably, controversial. However, he showed he had the character and mental strength to match his ability when he made his first

appearance as an Arsenal player against Tottenham Hotspur in November 2001. His impeccable display was the perfect answer to his critics, and he played with a calm authority that belied the emotionally charged atmosphere at White Hart Lane that day.

At season's end, Sol had helped Arsenal to the 'double'. He had explained when he joined the Club the previous July that: 'My decision was based on football... I felt this was the place to be.' They have proved prophetic words.

Sol continued to impress during his second season as an Arsenal player. He would miss the FA Cup final win against Southampton in May through suspension, but his contribution to another Cup success was not underestimated by his team-mates, least of all Martin Keown. 'He's been fantastic all season,' Keown told reporters just moments after the final whistle at the Millennium Stadium as he dedicated Arsenal's victory to the absent Sol.

Sol leaps highest after scoring against Newcastle, 2

The Contenders

Andy Linighan, 1990–1997
(118 appearances, 5 goals)

When Andy joined Arsenal for the 1990/91 season he walked into a squad containing established defenders such as David O'Leary, Tony Adams and Steve Bould. With O'Leary coming to the end of his long Highbury career, however, the former Norwich centre back obviously felt that his time would arrive. But Martin Keown was signed as the Irishman's replacement to ensure that Linighan would be remembered by Arsenal fans mainly as back up to the famous defence.

It was unfortunate that Linighan, an accomplished central defender in his own right, was at his peak at the same time as Adams, Bould and Keown. But he enjoyed his moment of glory in the FA Cup final replay against Sheffield Wednesday in 1993 when, despite having had his nose broken, he scored the vital extra-time goal which brought joy to London N5. He was also a member of Arsenal's 1993 League Cup-winning team that also triumphed over Wednesday.

After making over 150 appearances for Arsenal the popular defender opted for a move to Crystal Palace. Captain at Selhurst Park for a time, he was voted the club's player of the year in 2001 before finishing his League career at Oxford.

Herbie Roberts, 1926–1938
(333 appearances, 5 goals)

Herbie Roberts was Arsenal's first great defensive hero, and he was the player around whom Herbert Chapman built his revolutionary new third back game in the 1930s.

The 2–3–5 formation, which had been popular since the 1880s, was adapted by withdrawing the centre half into the defence and pushing the fullbacks out toward the flanks. The system became known as the 'WM' formation, or third back game.

The pivotal role in the new system was, of course, the centre half, and after much searching Chapman found the perfect man for this job in Roberts. He was not particularly skilful and he was reputed to be unable to kick the ball very far, but as a stopper he was peerless. He rarely ventured forward and seldom moved toward the flanks. Instead, he would patrol the centre of his own half, intercepting any balls played down the middle, heading them away or passing the ball short to a team-mate.

Tom Whittaker, the former Arsenal manager, once commented: 'Roberts's genius came from his intelligence and, even more important, that he did what he was told... Because he carried out his orders, his inability to kick a ball hard or far was camouflaged.'

Nose broken but unperturbed, Linighan heads home against Wednesday in 1993.

David Rocastle FACTFILE

272
Appearances

35
Goals

Born: Lewisham, London, 2 May 1967
Died: London, 31 March 2001
Joined Arsenal as a schoolboy in May 1982, turning pro in December 1984

Honours: League Championship 1988/89, 1990/91; Littlewoods Cup 1987
International Honours: 14 England caps

'He was a **bubbly character** with a lovely spirit, a fantastic spirit. Really, he was an Arsenal person.'

Paul Davis

David Rocastle was a footballer with that rarest and most valuable of gifts... the ability to entertain the crowd. He was, however, more than just a showman. He worked hard, played with discipline and did his defensive work. But when it was time to play, nobody played better than David. There was an impishness about his football that instantly endeared him to the Arsenal crowd. A shimmy one way, a feint the other, a little drag-back to put his opponent on his backside and David was away, with the North Bank cheering and his grounded adversary cursing. Small wonder that Highbury fell in love with David Rocastle.

Having risen through the Arsenal ranks alongside other emerging talents like Tony Adams, Michael Thomas and Paul Merson, he was recognized by management and team-mates alike as the most naturally gifted of the group. He was an integral part of George Graham's team which won the League Championship in 1988/89 and 1990/91 and former colleagues remain baffled as to why his career didn't go on to reach even greater heights.

In an Arsenal team renowned for its defensive obduracy, the dazzling dribbling skills of this perfectly balanced sportsman shone like a beacon, winning him many admirers as well as 14 England caps and a host of accolades.

Paul Davis, another product of the Arsenal youth Academy, remains one of David's biggest fans and says: 'He was an adventurous player, and the fans absolutely loved him. There were no airs and graces about him; he would speak to everyone the same. He was a fantastic guy to have known. He was a bubbly character with a lovely spirit, a fantastic spirit. Really, he was an Arsenal person. I always remember

He was an adventurous player, and the fans absolutely loved him. There were no airs and graces about him.

Paul Davis on his friend and former team-mate

84

A youthful looking Rocky shows off the 1987 League Cup trophy.

Dave had many great qualities, as we know, as a player but perhaps outsiders didn't appreciate how unselfish he was. He would do anything for the team.

Michael Thomas

when he left the Club, it was one of the saddest moments for him.

'Dave was somebody who the fans saw as a real Arsenal man, and that's exactly what he was. He gave everything in every game and the fans recognized that from early on. He also had fantastic skill and was naturally gifted with extremely quick feet. His game did change later on after he'd had a knee injury and the Club felt he was not the same player after that injury. It was a situation that definitely affected him. He was very strong-willed but like most of us he was sensitive to criticism. He could get over a lot of things but if certain people, like the manager, said things, it would affect him.

'I think it's fair to say that he never got back to the level he'd been at as an Arsenal player anywhere else. I spoke to him throughout his career and I never felt he was happy at any of his other clubs.'

Back in the late 1980s it had seemed inconceivable that David might leave the Club. He had made his debut in 1985/86, during Don Howe's final season in charge, and had established himself by the following season. The supporters were clearly taken with their new right winger, voting him Player of the Year in 1986. Two years later, and by now under George Graham's guidance, David was a key player in Arsenal's first Championship-winning team for 18 years. His progress was rewarded with an England debut against Denmark at Wembley in September 1988. After the game, he was asked how he would deal with his growing fame and status: 'The same way I've been dealing with it since I started with Arsenal. I'll just keep my head down, work hard, and remember the things that I'm good at.'

David proved as good as his word, and his consistently impressive performances saw him deservedly named as Barclay's Young Eagle of the Year in 1989. A second League Championship medal was clinched in 1991, with David overcoming both knee and toe injuries to play a vital role in a memorable season at Highbury. His form improved still further in 1991/92, with David switching position from the right flank to central midfield, and coming of age as a playmaker of both skill and enterprise. His growing maturity was evident in his comments to the Arsenal programme, 'I've often heard the cries from the crowd telling me to "go forward Rocky". I realize that's what the fans have come to expect. That's what I love to do. But sometimes you have to play a role for the team. Often that involves performing less eye-catching tasks.'

However, despite his selfless team-play and undoubted skill, David was considered surplus to requirements at Highbury in the summer of 1992 and he was sold to reigning champions Leeds United. Rocky's departure to Elland Road

David takes on a Newcastle defender as Gus Caesar looks on.

coincided roughly with Michael Thomas's move to Liverpool. Thomas and Rocastle had played in the same district side together, had come up through the Arsenal ranks together and, subsequently, shared the highs of Championship success.

Michael remembers the teenage Rocastle as being 'quiet, unassuming, but very sure of himself,' adding: 'Even though I played in the same district team as Dave, neither I nor any of our team-mates at the time knew that while he was still playing for us he had been training with Arsenal. He just never felt the need to tell anyone, maybe because he didn't want to appear big-headed. That was the sort of person he was. It was only when I told him I had been invited to train at Arsenal that he let the cat out of the bag and told me he'd been there for some time. Typically modest and one of the many things that made him such a wonderful person.'

As the pair progressed through the youth team and towards the senior side, Thomas says that David began to 'come out of his shell, much more so than I did.' Not that it changed him or his attitude towards the game, or those around him. Thomas explains: 'Dave had many great qualities, as we know, as a player but perhaps outsiders didn't appreciate how unselfish he was. He would do anything for the team. He would sacrifice his own job to help out a team-mate on the field and that's another reason why he had so much respect. When he was in possession he would hold the ball up for ages in order to allow team-mates to join up with the play, another example of his unselfish nature. I would just give him the ball and watch him go.'

He was a strong character on the pitch and in the dressing room. Away from the Club he was a wonderful person to be around. David was a wonderful talent... I thought he had the potential to be one of the greats who might have played 70 or 80 times for England.

Lee Chapman

The views of Lee Chapman, the former Arsenal striker who later became a team-mate of David's at Leeds, confirm that while Rocky wasn't as happy at Leeds as he had been at Highbury, the experience never changed him. He said: 'He was a strong character on the pitch and in the dressing room. Away from the Club he was a wonderful person to be around. David was a wonderful talent. He came to Leeds and showed glimpses of his best form, but I'm sure he'll be best remembered for his days at Arsenal. He still had a wonderful career, but I thought he had the potential to be one of the greats who might have played 70 or 80 times for England.'

After further truncated spells with Manchester City, Chelsea, Norwich and Hull (both on loan), David retired in January 2000 due to his recurring knee injury. Later that year he was diagnosed as suffering from non-Hodgkin's lymphoma – an aggressive form of cancer that attacks the immune system. Despite initial hope that he would recover, he sadly passed away on 31 March 2001.

Former team-mate Viv Anderson says: 'Of the talented youngsters who were coming through at the time I joined Arsenal in 1984 – Merson, Thomas, Adams and Rocastle – David was the most naturally gifted of them all. No disrespect to the others but he was fantastic on the ball, he could manipulate the ball and go past people for fun. Not only that but he was quick, athletic and strong – the perfect build for a footballer. Good looking too, the swine! In fact, he had the lot – all rolled up into one neat package. He excited people too, with his style of wing play, and was great for me to work with down the right side.'

Off the field, Viv remembers David as a 'smashing, smashing lad' who, while supremely confident in his own ability, was never cocky, always polite and always respectful of the older, more experienced players around him, even though he did insist on calling the experienced England full back 'Dad'! 'He had a great personality, he was a fantastic lad to have around the place and he was as honest as the day is long,' adds Viv. 'Although he had the lot, in terms of ability, he was always willing to learn, always prepared to listen to advice and take it on board.'

It seems that whoever you talk to about David Rocastle, everyone is unanimous in the view that his personality was as engaging as his natural ability. Brian Marwood, another admirer, reckons that David was 'just the player George Graham was looking for on the right-hand side' and was a possible catalyst for the success which was to follow. 'George really got the best out of him too,' recalls Marwood, who operated on the opposite flank in the late 1980s. 'I don't think I have ever seen anyone as skilful as David, either in training or in games, and George really worked at getting him to take the ability he had to punish people into match situations. He helped David harness all the skills he had.

'David was a very strong, athletic boy and a lovely person too. He's sadly missed. Pound for pound he was probably the most talented individual at that Football Club and it is hard to believe that his career didn't really progress the way it should have done after he left Arsenal. He was a very popular player at the Club too, and not just because of the ability he possessed. He had a lovely personality; he was always bright and effervescent and was a great character to have around the place. He had so much to look forward to in life and it was a tragedy that he was taken away so soon.'

Rocky demonstrates the poise and balance that made him an Arsenal legend.

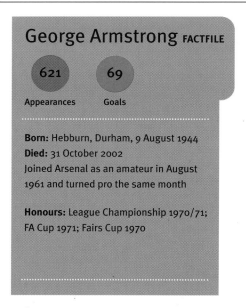

George Armstrong FACTFILE

621
Appearances

69
Goals

Born: Hebburn, Durham, 9 August 1944
Died: 31 October 2002
Joined Arsenal as an amateur in August
1961 and turned pro the same month

Honours: League Championship 1970/71;
FA Cup 1971; Fairs Cup 1970

> If he ever had to miss an Arsenal game through injury he was absolutely heartbroken. He lived for the game but he was also a great family man as well.

Frank McLintock

The Runner-up

George Armstrong was unquestionably one of the most popular figures in the history of Arsenal Football Club. His reputation as a kind-hearted, warm and generous man went before him. He was, quite simply, liked by everybody. However, aside from being a thoroughly good man, it should not be forgotten that George was also a fine footballer. His modest demeanour and complete lack of arrogance belied the fact that he was a true Arsenal great who enjoyed a long career of high achievement at Highbury.

George was an industrious yet skilful midfielder; a willing worker who gave his all to the team cause and whose accurate crossing became a vital factor in Arsenal's successes under Bertie Mee. He would later put many of these qualities to good use as a valued member of the Highbury coaching staff, assisting first George Graham and later Arsène Wenger in the 1990s.

It was, however, on 24 August 1961, during George Swindin's managerial reign, that the young Armstrong first arrived in London N5 from his native North-East (hence the nickname 'Geordie'). Within six months, the 17-year-old winger had made his first-team debut in a League match against

Blackpool, and by season's end, he had made three more appearances and scored one goal too. It was the start of a glorious Arsenal career that would see Armstrong make a further 496 League appearances before departing for a brief spell at Leicester City in 1977. Along the way, the likeable winger collected winners' medals for his part in the 1970/71 'double' and the previous season's Fairs Cup triumph.

A measure of his supreme fitness and consistency was the fact that he started every game of the 1969/70 season, 64 in all, and was rewarded by being named the Club's player of the year.

The pinnacle of his career was, of course, the 1971 'double', although Bob Wilson – a friend of George's for 37 years – remembers him producing 'one of his greatest ever performances' in the second leg of the 1970 Fairs Cup final against Anderlecht when Arsenal overturned a 3–1 deficit from the first leg with a 3–0 victory at Highbury to win the Cup. It was the sort of display which Wilson believes should have earned Armstrong more than youth and Under-23 honours on the international scene: 'The fact that he never played for England is a disgrace to every England team selection ever made.

'He was unbelievable in the air and had a beautiful touch on the ball. The modern equivalent would be Edu, a player who doesn't necessarily have the pace of some of his contemporaries but has an incredible footballing brain and also puts his foot in. George had a great career at Arsenal; he was there as a kid and he never wanted to go anywhere else. Obviously he came back as a coach and he died on the training field, in effect. He should go down as one of the greatest Arsenal players of all time.

'He ploughed up and down the left wing but if you wanted him to come inside he'd do that; he was an amazingly energetic player. Right to the end of his life he had great energy and incredible talent to go with it. His ability to cross the ball was fantastic. We used to have a board on which we would record goals and assists, and Geordie's name was constantly on that board. It would read "assist – Armstrong, assist – Armstrong".

'We loved him like no other because he was the most generous little devil you've ever seen.

He'd knock you out of the way to get to the bar. He was an extraordinary guy. Nobody ever had a bad word to say about him.'

Armstrong returned to Highbury during the reign of his former team-mate Graham in 1990, assuming responsibility for Arsenal's reserves, and he continued in this role under Bruce Rioch and Wenger. However, on 31 October 2000, at the age of just 56, George died of a brain haemorrhage. It was a tragedy that left Arsenal's playing and coaching staff stunned. Arsène Wenger summed the mood up succinctly, 'Losing Geordie has been a massive blow to everybody... he was a true Arsenal man, a real symbol of the Club.'

Frank McLintock, captain of the 'double'-winning team of 1971 in which George was an ever-present, said: 'This has shattered me because I can honestly not remember him having a day's illness all the time I knew him. If he ever had to miss an Arsenal game through injury he was absolutely heartbroken.'

George strains every sinew as he sprints down the wing against Chelsea.

Freddie Ljungberg FACTFILE

183
Appearances

31
Goals

Born: Halmstad, Sweden, 16 April 1977
Joined Arsenal from Halmstad in
September 1998

Honours: League Championship
2001/02; FA Cup 2002, 2003
International Honours: 36 Sweden caps

Third Place

**What better way to endear yourself to the
Highbury faithful than to mark your Arsenal debut
with a beautifully executed lob over Peter
Schmeichel in a 3–0 win against Manchester
United? Step forward Freddie Ljungberg, a player
with an incomparable ability to score decisive and
dramatic goals. The 21-year-old Swede, who had
been on the field for just minutes prior to his *coup
de grâce* against Schmeichel, was an instant hero
with the Highbury faithful. It is a status he has
frequently lived up to in the following seasons.**

In truth, Arsène Wenger had not expected
Freddie to make his mark so early. Wenger used
his new Scandinavian midfielder sparingly during
1998/99, but by the following season he could hold
back Freddie no longer. Six goals in 26 Premiership
appearances – including home and away goals
against Manchester United – was an impressive
return, but it was merely a foretaste of what was
to come.

The 5ft 9in Swede can operate on either flank or
through the middle and, while he is tenacious
enough, it is his attacking play that is truly
remarkable. Freddie is a player who is constantly
thinking, constantly on the look out for an

opportunity to dart forward. He'll calmly drop off
the shoulder of his marker, appearing to be moving
away from danger and then, when his opponent is
out of sight, he'll make his move forward. It is a
routine that he repeats endlessly throughout
matches. Sometimes his marker tracks him and on
other occasions a pass is not forthcoming, but
Freddie is unperturbed. The darting runs continue,
causing havoc and creating space for others.

Freddie is also a player who is nerveless in front
of goal; he never hesitates and has been blessed
by a striker's ability to see the goal rather than the
goalkeeper before him. His goalscoring potential
was never more clearly demonstrated than during
the 2001/02 'double' season. Freddie scored seven
times in seven games during the Championship
run-in, ending the season with 12 League goals. He
was also a Cup-final scorer for the second season
running, netting with a fine curling shot around
Chelsea keeper Carlo Cudicini. Injuries would
hinder Freddie throughout much of the following
season, although he was back in the team for
another Cup final at the Millennium Stadium. This
time he did not score, although it was his shot that
ricocheted to Robert Pires for the game's only goal.

Golden boy with red hair... Freddie celebrates a goal.

The Contenders

Ray Parlour, 1988–present
(429 appearances, 22 goals)

Having been introduced to the first team as a teenager by George Graham, Parlour made a difficult debut in a 2–0 defeat at Anfield in January 1992, and served notice of his enormous potential some weeks later when he scored his first senior Arsenal goal in only his second full game.

He continued to make 20-plus appearances a season throughout the 1990s, enjoying his best campaign during the title-winning 1997/98 season, when he contributed five goals from 34 League appearances although missing out on the FA Cup final victory against Newcastle.

Through determination and hard work he had become an integral part of a midfield unit which then included World Cup winners Patrick Vieira and Emmanuel Petit, and his contributions over the next few seasons were crucial, a fact not overlooked by England boss Glenn Hoddle who awarded him the first of ten international caps to date.

Even now, despite amassing more than 400 first-team appearances, Parlour continues to have to fight for his place. But Ray can always be relied on to put in a whole-hearted 90 minutes, supported by the composure he has gained with the benefit of experience.

Michael Thomas, 1982–1991
(196 appearances, 24 goals)

Arsenal fans who have enjoyed countless re-runs of Michael's title-winning goal at Anfield in 1989 may be surprised to learn that the raiding fullback who became a midfield dynamo on George Graham's instruction can hardly bear to sit through replays. A reserved individual whose confidence on the field belied his natural shyness, Michael has been known to leave the room while clips of his goal are shown.

'It was an incredible night, a wonderful moment I still find hard to describe, but I am a little embarrassed when it comes on the TV and there are people around,' he confesses. 'People might think I've watched the video a million times, but I haven't. When it comes on it's normally my cue for a sharp exit.'

But he was delighted to accept the acclaim of his former team-mates when invited back to Highbury to receive his second Championship winners' medal, following the 1990/91 triumph, having departed for Liverpool during the season. Michael, who will always be something of a Highbury hero because of his goal at Anfield, smiles as he recalls his Arsenal return: 'I got a standing ovation when I went up to collect my medal.' It was the least he deserved.

Ray opens the scoring against Chelsea in the 2001 FA Cup final.

Liam Brady FACTFILE

295
Appearances

59
Goals

Born: Dublin, 13 February 1956
Joined Arsenal as an apprentice in
August 1973

Honours: FA Cup 1979
International Honours: 72 Republic of
Ireland caps

'The **greatest left foot** that has
ever been at the Arsenal.'

Charlie George

Lightly built and of average height, the young Liam Brady cut an unconvincing figure among the hurly-burly of First Division midfield action in the mid-1970s. In an era of muddy pitches, thundering tackles and lenient refereeing, physical stature was a valuable commodity but it was one that Liam did not possess. What he did possess in abundance, however, was talent and that, allied to both vision and intelligence, kept the youngster at the heart of the action but out of range of opponents. Liam's greatest asset was his left foot, which conjured a seemingly endless succession of goals and assists during the Dubliner's seven seasons in the Arsenal first team.

Liam, who hails from Dublin's north side, comes from a footballing family and it soon became evident that he had grown up around the game. Uncle Frank had been a member of the first ever Republic of Ireland team in 1926, while brothers Ray and Paddy had played for Millwall and QPR, so it came as no great surprise to the other Bradys that Liam took up an apprenticeship at Arsenal upon leaving school.

However, in his early days at Highbury many were concerned that Liam's lack of physical stature might hinder his progress. The suggestion was that the wiry youngster would not be able to cope in the competitive environs of the First Division. The Club attempted to beef up the teenage Brady but their efforts made little difference. According to folklore, Liam was invariably to be found with his nose in a bag of chips during this period; presumably it was hoped fried potatoes might make him gain that all-important bulk. In fact, all it did was lead to Liam earning the nickname 'Chippy'.

> Liam could put international defenders on their backsides with a sway of the hips and he has such a great football brain.
>
> Kenny Sansom

Joe Jordan (left) and Lou Macari (right) watch as Liam bursts forward at Wembley in 1979.

Whatever the coaching staff's reservations about Liam's physique, they could not ignore his talent and in 1973, aged 17, he was handed his first-team debut by Bertie Mee. The young Irishman played for the first time in a First Division match against Birmingham City, coming on for the injured Jeff Blockley in a 1–0 victory over the Midlanders. Liam stole the show, making an indelible mark upon the minds of watching Arsenal fans.

By the start of the 1974/75 season Liam had established himself in Mee's line-up, forming an exciting midfield combination with Alan Ball. The England World Cup winner proved an excellent mentor for the emergent Brady and the Irishman showed a voracious appetite for learning, constantly improving his game alongside the former Evertonian. Of course, much of Liam's football was natural. It would have been impossible to teach him the kind of balance and poise that gave the Dubliner such assured control of the ball, just as it would be futile to attempt to teach somebody to play with the kind of vision or innovative spirit that truly set Brady apart.

However, even for a player of Liam Brady's considerable talent, the Arsenal team of the mid-1970s was not an ideal place for an emergent playmaker to show his skills. The team was in a state of transition, with Bertie Mee still trying to rebuild his playing staff following the inevitable decline of the 1970/71 'double' team. Liam's first two seasons as a first-team regular both ended with the Gunners perilously close to the relegation zone, in 16th and 17th place in the First Division.

Throughout this difficult period, much responsibility fell on the shoulders of Mee's three midfield staples, Brady, Ball and George Armstrong. Ball and Armstrong, of course, had the benefit of years of experience in top-flight football, but for Liam, Arsenal's situation offered a profound challenge. It soon became clear that the lightly built Irishman had an inner strength that exceeded his physical size and he rapidly showed himself to be a player of substance as much as style. Liam, perhaps learning from his international skipper Johnny Giles who was similar in stature, never ducked a challenge and was rarely shaken off the ball once in possession. But the quality that his team-mates admired most was his willingness to accept possession no matter how closely marked and in any position. Hiding was not in Brady's nature.

'Brady as a footballer was quite unique, with his intelligence, control of the ball, accuracy and eye for an opening, he read the game so well,' says former

 The fact that he played for seven years in Italy tells you how good he was.

Joe Baker

Liam wheels away in delight after a goal against Sheffield United in 1976.

Arsenal legend Joe Baker, adding: 'And there have been few better left foots.'

Liam's famous left foot would take on even more importance for Arsenal following the departure of Alan Ball to Southampton in 1976. The apprentice was now given centre stage. It was an opportunity that Liam was ready for and he seemed to thrive on the additional responsibility which inevitably came his way.

In 1978 Arsenal reached their first Cup final for six years thanks in no small part to the contribution of the 22-year-old Liam. Alas, an injury to the inspirational midfielder saw him in unusually subdued mood in the final. He was eventually substituted and Arsenal lost 1–0 to Ipswich Town. A year later Liam and his team-mates made amends, with the playmaker giving arguably his most memorable performance in an Arsenal jersey.

Brady, whose two goals had helped Terry Neill's team negotiate a tricky third-round tie against Sheffield Wednesday, was in inspired form during the first half of the FA Cup final against Manchester United. At the interval Arsenal led 2–0, but two scrappy United goals in five second-half minutes threatened to undermine the good work. With time running out, Arsenal kicked off after United's equalizer and, as usual, the ball wound up at Brady's feet. The Irishman strode forward – as much in an effort to run down the clock as anything else – and slid an inch-perfect pass into the path of Graham Rix who crossed for Alan Sunderland to slot home one of the most memorable goals in Cup history. After his consummate display, it was only fitting that Liam should have played a major role in the winning game.

However, the Cup final celebrations had barely begun to die down when the announcement came that Liam would be leaving Highbury at the end of the 1979/80 season. His contract was due to expire and he was eager to find a new challenge, with a move to Juventus in Serie A his eventual destination. 'I told Liam not to go to Italy,' recalls John Radford. 'I said they would kick him off the park. It's lucky he didn't take my advice because he probably came back a millionaire.'

Liam would definitely get into the current Arsenal team, there is no doubt about that.

Alan Skirton

The bad news was at least tempered by the knowledge that the Highbury faithful would be treated to one last season of Brady magic. And Liam's farewell campaign was nothing if not eventful. A goal against Brighton in a 4–0 win at the Goldstone Ground on opening day signalled his intention to leave on a high, and he produced a succession of exceptional performances in a season that saw Arsenal finish in a respectable fourth place in the League, while making even more memorable progress in Cup competitions.

Liam missed just one game en route to a third successive FA Cup final, playing a full role in an epic four-match semi-final win against Liverpool, but at Wembley he and his team-mates were frustrated by West Ham United's cautious tactics and lost 1–0. Four days later Liam ended his Arsenal career at the Heysel Stadium in Brussels against Valencia in the European Cup Winners' Cup final. It proved another defensive encounter, in which Liam was given little opportunity to shine. A penalty shoot-out decided the contest in the Spaniards' favour.

Arsenal had won through to the Cup Winners' Cup final with a 2–1 aggregate victory over Juventus. Ironically, Liam was at his irrepressible best against his future employers, taking control of midfield and making a mockery of the Turin club's status as overwhelming favourites to reach the final. It was a performance, no doubt, that reassured the Italian giants that they were getting a player of genuine quality.

Liam was still just 24 and it would not be easy to find a ready-made replacement. How do you replace a player whom Charlie George describes as possessing 'the greatest left foot that has ever been at the Arsenal.'

Brady for his part, quickly made an impact on Serie A. 'Liam emphasized just what a great player he was by his success with Juventus,' says George. In two seasons in Turin, Liam was twice a champion. Two seasons at Sampdoria and another two at Inter Milan followed, before Liam joined his last Italian club, Ascoli, in 1986. When he returned to England in March 1987, he had made 189 Serie A appearances and had cost combined transfer fees reported to be in excess of £3m. Joe Baker, who himself played in Italy with Torino, believes Liam's Italian record reveals his true quality. 'The fact that he played for seven years in Italy tells you how good he was,' says Baker. 'For those were the days of the *catenaccio* defences when you were kicked if you breathed.'

Much to the eternal disappointment of Arsenal fans, Liam signed for West Ham United rather than Arsenal when he returned to England. However, his decision to avoid a return to the scene of his former glories – something which many players are eager to do – has had no bearing on his status as a Highbury legend. In any case, after three years in East London Liam hung up his boots.

Initially, the 34-year-old Brady embarked upon a career as a players' agent, but when the job of Celtic manager became available he switched tack. However, his tenure at Celtic Park proved ill-fated, coinciding with a traumatic period in the club's history, and he soon moved on. A spell in charge at Brighton followed, but once more Liam found himself at a club in difficult circumstances and he again moved on. Thankfully, this time he returned to the familiar environs of Highbury, taking up the role of head of youth development in 1996.

It is as a skilful and visionary midfield playmaker that Liam Brady will always be remembered at the Club. The final word goes to another former Arsenal man, Alan Skirton, who watched in awe at Brady's dominance of First Division midfields in the 1970s: 'My little idol he was. A wonderfully balanced player, not especially quick but with the ability to go past people as if they weren't there... Liam and Geordie Armstrong would definitely get into the current Arsenal team, there is no doubt about that.'

Liam was the architect of all three Arsenal goals during the 1979 FA Cup final.

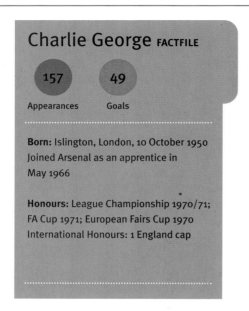

Charlie George FACTFILE

157 Appearances

49 Goals

Born: Islington, London, 10 October 1950
Joined Arsenal as an apprentice in
May 1966

Honours: League Championship 1970/71;
FA Cup 1971; European Fairs Cup 1970
International Honours: 1 England cap

'We had gifted
players, but we had just
one free spirit... and that
was Charlie. '

Bob Wilson on the 1970/71 'double' team

The Runner-up

Try saying 'Charlie George' without saying 'darling of the North Bank'. It's not easy. **Charlie was of course not just the darling of the North Bank, he was beloved by the Clock End and both stands, too. In short, he was the perfect Highbury hero. He was a local boy, a stylish character and, best of all, he was an exciting and skilful footballer. If you add in his penchant for scoring memorable goals, it's easy to see why Arsenal Football Club fell in love with Charlie George.**

Charlie had been an Arsenal supporter in his youth and his passion for the Club was obvious. He arrived as an apprentice in 1966 and found himself making his first-team debut aged 18 two years later. His was a rapid ascent through the ranks but Charlie's talent had been difficult to ignore.

He had searing pace, effortless control, sublime balance and a devastating shot, a package that at times came close to perfection. But what truly set him apart was his swagger. Charlie was a cavalier footballer who did everything with a flourish. Shots were curled or chipped, defenders were teased with feints and drag-backs and his goals were invariably spectacular. Bertie Mee drafted in the young Charlie during the 1969/70 season, playing him in attack

alongside John Radford. The fledgling striker clocked up an impressive total of 28 League appearances that season and his total would have been higher but for a sending-off that resulted in a suspension and a spell in the reserves.

Charlie soon won back his place, however, and he played a full part in Arsenal's European Fairs Cup final win over Anderlecht, so ending his debut season with a major European trophy.

The following year would bring greater glory for both Charlie George and Arsenal, although it has to be said that the early signs were not encouraging. In the first game of the season, Charlie broke an ankle as he collided with Everton keeper Gordon West in the act of scoring at Goodison Park. By the New Year he had recovered but with Ray Kennedy in impressive form alongside Radford, Charlie was unable to win back his place up front. Instead, Mee and Don Howe decided to move him back into midfield. It proved a masterstroke.

'I always thought Charlie was best just behind the two strikers,' says former team-mate Bob Wilson. 'Let him come on to the play from deep, drift in and out of the game.' Wilson adds that 'We [the 1970/71 'double' team] had gifted players, many of whom had made themselves technically correct through hours of hardwork, but we had just one free spirit... and that was Charlie.'

Charlie quickly made the most of his new opportunity, terrorizing opposition defences with his intelligent passing and powerful shooting. As Arsenal marched towards the 'double', his goals were particularly valuable in the FA Cup. It was Charlie who opened the scoring at Maine Road with a free-kick that gave Joe Corrigan no chance in the City goal and earned Arsenal's passage to the sixth round. He was then on target in the quarter-final against Leicester City. However, the goal he is most remembered for came a few weeks later.

The setting was Wembley, the FA Cup final the prize. The match was in extra time with the score at 1–1, legs were weary and the tension intolerable. A visibly exhausted Charlie George, who had been pushed up front by Don Howe, collected a pass from Radford and crashed a thunderous 20-yard shot past Ray Clemence in the Liverpool goal. The stadium erupted as players everywhere collapsed and Charlie threw out his arms and fell on his back in a now legendary celebration. It was a goal worthy of any Cup final and it clinched the 'double'.

The man in goal for Arsenal in that Wembley final was Bob Wilson, and the former Gunner is fulsome in his praise of his ex-team-mate. 'Charlie was a fantastic passer of the ball – people think of Charlie for the spectacular goals, and he could drill one in from 25 yards and you could play him up front as a striker, but Raddy [John Radford] and Ray Kennedy were the perfect partnership and Charlie was ideal in the 'Dennis Bergkamp' role just behind them.

'He could drill balls right or left, he could switch the play and he could take a great free-kick. He was born to be a footballer, he was a rascal but he was the only free spirit in our team.'

Charlie remained a significant force in the Arsenal team for the next four seasons but his form never regained the heights of 1970/71. A persistent knee problem did not aid the situation, and in the summer of 1975 the darling of the North Bank departed for Derby County, to the disappointment of all those who had so idolized him.

Charlie makes light of a boggy seventies pitch and heads for goal.

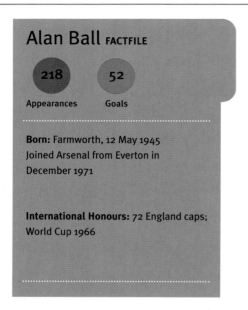

Alan Ball FACTFILE

218
Appearances

52
Goals

Born: Farmworth, 12 May 1945
Joined Arsenal from Everton in
December 1971

International Honours: 72 England caps;
World Cup 1966

Third Place

**When Bertie Mee signed Alan Ball from Everton
in 1971 it seemed that the Arsenal manager had
made the perfect acquisition. The energetic
midfielder had already won the World Cup with
England five years earlier, but at just 26 years
old, he was still approaching his peak. It was a
bold statement of ambition from Mee, who
added Ball to a squad that had won the 'double'
just a few months previously. Alas, though
individually Alan was a success at Highbury, his
five-year stay coincided with a decline in the
team's fortunes, and he departed without
collecting any further major honours.**

Mee had made his move for Ball after watching
his team make an indifferent start to their title
defence. Alan was a midfielder of energy and
enterprise, a player who could unpick defences
with a slick pass but who would also be willing to
run the length of the pitch to make a last-ditch
tackle. His was also an inspirational presence and
he was an expert at getting the best from those
around him.

Ball's arrival at Highbury prompted an upturn in
form that took in a nine-match unbeaten run, and
he also helped his new team to reach the FA Cup
final for the second season in succession.
However, that game against Leeds proved a
disappointment, ending in a 1–0 defeat.

The following season Alan came to the fore
as a major player at Arsenal and his influence
helped Mee's team to finish as runners-up to
Liverpool in the First Division. Despite the
impressive League showing, it was clear that
Arsenal were a side in transition. The 'double'
team was rapidly dispersing – Graham had
left, and McLintock, Kennedy and George
would soon follow – and the likes of Liam
Brady and Frank Stapleton were not yet ready
to replace them.

Inevitably, more responsibility was heaped on
Alan Ball's shoulders and in 1973 he was made
captain. He took charge of a side short on
confidence and light on quality. Ball did his best
to inspire the team, but in his last full season at
Highbury, Arsenal finished in a lowly 17th place.
Alan, who scored nine goals in 1975/76, had
contributed significantly to a season that might
have ended in relegation. However, after the
appointment of Terry Neill as manager Alan left
for Southampton in December 1976.

Alan lets fly with a long-distance shot.

The Contenders

George Graham, 1966–1972
(296 appearances, 77 goals)

One of Bertie Mee's first signings as Arsenal manager, Graham joined the Club from Chelsea in September 1966, going on to star in both the Fairs Cup success of 1970 and the following season's 'double' triumph.

At Chelsea, George had been a prolific centre forward, scoring 35 times in 72 appearances, and he began his Highbury career as a striker, scoring on his debut against Leicester City at Highbury. But although Graham was top scorer in each of his first two seasons at Arsenal, Mee made the bold decision to switch him to midfield in 1969. It proved an inspired move, with Graham revelling in his new role as playmaker.

George was able to reveal a range of creative talents and his greatest weakness, a lack of pace, was no longer an issue. He remained a potent attacking threat, due in no small part to his aerial ability, and scored 11 times in the League during the 1970/71 'double' season, although perhaps his most important goal was saved for the FA Cup semi-final replay against Stoke City.

At the age of 28 George was sold to Manchester United in the winter of 1972. He would, of course, return to Highbury as manager in the 1980s.

George Eastham, 1960–1966
(223 appearances, 41 goals)

George Eastham will for ever be remembered as the man who caused the abolition of the old 'retain and transfer' system, thereby revolutionizing footballers' pay and conditions. However, it should not be forgotten that he was a footballer of the highest quality.

The PFA and both clubs spent six months trying to resolve his drawn-out and expensive transfer from Newcastle to Arsenal and inevitably, after such tension and such a long lay-off, it took Eastham time to settle. The critics were quick to judge him after the furore over his move.

Thankfully, form and confidence soon returned, and the Blackpool-born inside forward began to make his mark. Though never a strong tackler, as a creative force he was peerless: able to dictate the pace of a game, he was particularly adept at linking up with his wingers, while through balls cunningly slipped between defenders were a speciality.

Eastham's stay at Highbury, however, coincided with a barren period in terms of silverware. George brought his spell at Arsenal to a close with a move to Stoke City in 1966.

George Graham claims Arsenal's equalizer in the 1971 Cup final.

Thierry Henry FACTFILE

205 Appearances

82 Goals

Born: Paris, France, 17 August 1977
Joined Arsenal from Juventus in
August 1999

Honours: League Championship 2001/02;
FA Cup 2002, 2003
International Honours: 46 France caps;
World Cup 1998; European Championship
2000; Confederations Cup 2003

'At the beginning I had to learn the role.

When I had chances, I was putting them in the back of the

stand rather than the back of the net. Now they're

going in more and more.'

Thierry Henry on the switch to centre forward

The very best players are never defined by their positions on the field. George Best was neither winger nor inside forward; Franz Beckenbauer was neither stopper nor midfielder; and Thierry Henry is similarly elusive when it comes to traditional labels. The French World Cup winner was once a winger, but he now operates nominally as a central striker although he remains far from the stereotypical number nine. However, while there may be disagreement about how best to describe Thierry's position, what is in no doubt is his considerable talent and devastating ability to tear apart opposing defences.

It seems unthinkable today, but when the former Monaco striker arrived at Highbury in the summer of 1999 from Juventus, many pundits doubted Arsène Wenger's wisdom for investing heavily in a player who had scored only four League goals in each of his previous two seasons. Like Dennis Bergkamp and Patrick Vieira before him, Thierry had struggled to make a major impact during his brief sojourn in Italy's Serie A and the move to Arsenal offered him the chance to resurrect his career in the Premiership. And, just like his team-mates, it was an opportunity of which he would make full use.

Somewhat ironically, Thierry's arrival at Arsenal coincided with the departure of his good friend and France team-mate Nicolas Anelka. Arsène Wenger was acutely aware of the comparisons that would be drawn between the two players but was confident in the quality of his new signing. 'Thierry has the ability to do as well as Nicolas,' explained the Arsenal manager, 'he has all the qualities, best of all is his pace and power dribbling.'

Anyone not entirely sure what 'power dribbling' was, would have been left in no

> He's like a Rolls-Royce when he goes past people.
>
> Bob Wilson on the pace and power of Thierry Henry

Fabien Barthez is caught out by Henry at Highbury in November 2001.

doubt by the end of the 1999/2000 season after watching Henry give numerous demonstrations. For a powerfully built man of 6ft 2in, the Parisian has extraordinary balance, and it is this quality allied to an assured touch on the ball and fantastic acceleration that makes him such a threat when running at defenders. He can twist and jink, making space for himself with a trick or a clever turn, but when shown clear grass ahead he is uncatchable, as many Premiership defenders have found to their cost over the past few seasons.

It is not clear whether Wenger signed Henry as a winger or as a player he could mould into a central striker, but however he intended to deploy him, it was soon evident that the Arsenal manager had bought a footballer of immense potential. The two men had previously worked together at Monaco so knew all about one another, but in any case Henry's pedigree was undeniable despite his difficult season with Juventus. Wenger had given Henry his first-team debut for Monaco back in 1994 and had watched his prodigy emerge from the French Under-18 team, which he captained, to become Young Footballer of the Year in 1997 and a senior international a year later. At the age of 20 he had won the World Cup with France, top-scoring for Aimé Jacquet's side in the 1998 finals. The credentials were all there, but the big question was whether Thierry could make an impact in the uniquely demanding environment of the Premiership.

Initially, the Frenchman found himself playing on the left flank of Arsenal's attack, while fellow new signing Davor Suker competed with Dennis Bergkamp and Kanu for the two central positions. Early signs were encouraging, his fleet-footed wing play impressive. However, it was still not clear where Thierry's favourite position was, and six goalless appearances offered little hint of the prolific performer who would soon come to the fore. It was not until late November that he finally had an extended run in the team as a central attacker, but when his chance came he made his mark in emphatic fashion. Nine goals in nine games was enough to make the rest of the Premiership take notice.

Arsenal ended the season as runners-up in the Premiership and lost to Galatasaray on penalties in the final of the UEFA Cup. For Thierry Henry, however, it had been a seminal campaign. His confidence was high once more and he had scored 26 goals in all competitions, making a mockery of his pre-Arsenal career statistics which suggested he was no more than an occasional scorer. Goals in London Derbies against both Tottenham and Chelsea at Highbury had, in particular, done much to endear the Frenchman to the Arsenal crowd.

Buoyed by his debut season at Highbury, Thierry enhanced his reputation still further by starring alongside Club mate Patrick Vieira and soon-to-be colleagues Robert Pires and Sylvain Wiltord for the victorious France team at the Euro 2000 Championships in Belgium and Holland. The young Frenchman was no longer Wenger's secret weapon, and pundits began to question how he would fare in his second season in England, the suggestion being that defenders would now know what to expect. However, four goals in the first four Premiership games of the 2000/01 campaign soon gave the answer.

Thierry's own expectations were growing, as demonstrated by his post-match comments after his winning performance against Manchester United in October. Flicking the ball up impudently on the edge of the United penalty area, he had

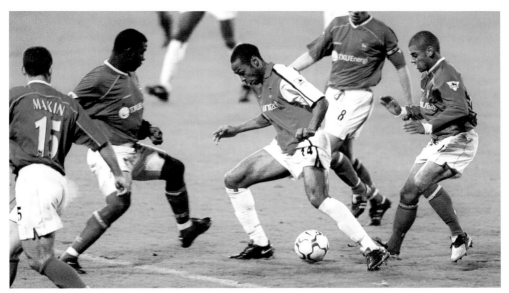

Ipswich defenders swarm around Thierry as he closes in on goal.

dispatched a breathtaking volley past Fabien Barthez to give Arsenal a 1–0 victory. 'I was a bit down because I haven't scored lately,' explained the striker, whose barren run had lasted for just three Premiership games.

For the remainder of the campaign Thierry continued to find the net with regularity and assurance. He ended as Arsenal's leading scorer for the second season running and counted France's Footballer of the Year among a host of recent awards and accolades. Still to win a major trophy for Arsenal, he could also consider himself unlucky not to have emerged from the Millennium Stadium with a winners' medal after the 2001 FA Cup final against Liverpool. Though Arsenal took the lead through Freddie Ljungberg, the game was eventually decided in Liverpool's favour by two late goals.

The frustrations of the 2001 Cup Final were, however, soon forgotten when Arsenal claimed a third League and FA Cup 'double' the following season. It was a campaign that the Club in general and Thierry Henry in particular enjoyed immensely. Fifteen Premiership goals in the first 15 games saw Thierry establish himself as the country's leading marksman, and it was his two goals in a 3–1 win against Manchester United in November at Highbury that gave Arsenal's Championship challenge a welcome boost. Robert Pires recalls that the United game 'changed things around' and that 'Thierry was outstanding.'

The Pires–Henry combination would be behind much of Arsenal's excellent attacking play during the 2001/02 'double' season. It was a partnership that owed much to the duo's complementary skills on the pitch and to their friendship off it. 'Titi is a friend and I owe him a lot,' explained Pires in his autobiography *Robert Pires Footballeur*, 'he opened my eyes to London, to Arsenal, and took me on board as his mate... He's gone out of his way to make me feel welcome.'

Henry's goals – many of which were of the spectacular variety – continued to flow at a prodigious rate. Long-distance curlers, volleys, chips… Arsenal's number fourteen demonstrated his full repertoire of goalscoring techniques in that 'double' year. One 25-yard free-kick in the Champions League match against Juventus capped an impeccable performance by Thierry against his former employers.

At the season's end, he had scored 32 times in 49 appearances, bringing his Arsenal career total to 80 goals in 140 games. It was a feat that deservingly brought Thierry the Premiership's Golden Boot as the League's top scorer and the Carling-Opta Player of the Season award. The following season brought still more goals and glory and in January 2003 he completed a century of goals for Arsenal with a brace against Birmingham City at St Andrews. It was an appropriate moment for Thierry to reflect on his first three seasons at Highbury.

'When Arsène first played me at centre forward a lot of people were asking what he was thinking of,' recalled the Frenchman. 'They have the answer now and it's the best answer you could have. At the beginning I had to learn to play the role. When I had chances, I was putting the ball in the back of the stand, rather than the back of the net. Now they're going in more and more.'

Arsène Wenger is rightly proud of Henry's achievements since he brought him to the Club in 1999. 'I think he is a fantastic striker – the exception becomes the norm with him,' explained the Arsenal manager upon hearing the news that Thierry had been named PFA Player of the Year in 2003. 'He's only 25 and has played just three years in this position,' continued Wenger. 'But what I like about him is that he is not only a goalscorer but also a team player who provides chances for other players as well.'

No Premiership player created more goals than Thierry in 2002/03, with the Frenchman credited with a record-breaking 20 assists. He frequently leads counter-attacks with dashing runs down the left flank, while his corners have been a source of goals, too. However, it is his running with the ball that seems to cause most terror in opposing defenders. Thierry's dribbling skills allied to his prodigious goalscoring ability were, no doubt, behind the decision of the Football Writers' Association to name him their player of 2003. It was an award that completed a rare Footballer of the Year double for the Arsenal man.

Final word on Thierry goes to Dennis Bergkamp, a player who after a career with Ajax, Inter Milan, his country, Holland and Arsenal, is well placed to judge fellow strikers. 'If you look at him and the whole package, with everything he's got, I don't think you can find that anywhere else in football,' said the Dutchman. 'He can go all the way and he'll become a legend. It's only taken him three years [to score 100 goals] and that's amazing.'

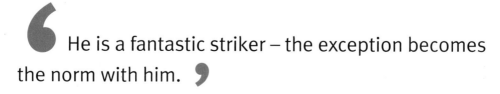

He is a fantastic striker – the exception becomes the norm with him.

Arsène Wenger

> If you look at him and the whole package, with everything he's got, I don't think you can find that anywhere else in football.

Denis Bergkamp

Thierry gets off the ground to cross with an overhead kick against Blackburn in 2002.

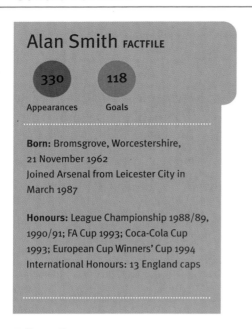

Alan Smith FACTFILE

330 Appearances

118 Goals

Born: Bromsgrove, Worcestershire, 21 November 1962
Joined Arsenal from Leicester City in March 1987

Honours: League Championship 1988/89, 1990/91; FA Cup 1993; Coca-Cola Cup 1993; European Cup Winners' Cup 1994
International Honours: 13 England caps

> ❛ Alan Smith is so easy to play with… He's so unselfish. He'll always create chances, besides scoring himself. ❜
>
> Ian Wright

The Runner-up

When Alan Smith volleyed home the winning goal in the 1994 Cup Winners' Cup final against Parma, many Arsenal fans were left pinching themselves in disbelief. Extravagant volleyed goals from the edge of the area were not the staple fare of a player more renowned for his intelligent team-play and unselfish front-running. But though many were surprised at Alan's feat on that night in Copenhagen, none begrudged the Midlander his moment of glory.

Smith arrived at Highbury in the spring of 1987 and had already contributed to two League Championship successes, and the FA Cup triumph of 1993, prior to his match-winning show against Parma. He was signed from Leicester City, but a delay in his registration meant his transfer missed the March deadline and so he spent the remainder of the 1986/87 season back on loan at Filbert Street. Once *in situ* as an Arsenal player, however, Alan was quickly on the goal trail, opening his account with a hat-trick against Portsmouth in the fourth League fixture of the season. Goals became harder to come by in mid-season, but by the end of the campaign Alan's confidence was back. He scored in both the League Cup semi-final and the Wembley showdown with Luton Town, which ended in a 3–2 defeat for George Graham's men.

Alan was top scorer in his first season at Highbury, as he would be for each of the next three years. The most prolific of his four golden seasons came in 1988/89, when Arsenal won the Championship for the first time in 18 years. Alan netted 24 times in 36 appearances, a remarkable strike rate, particularly for a player who was more than just a penalty-box poacher. 'He was excellent at holding the ball up but he also got his fair share of goals from crosses and the like,' remembers former team-mate Paul Davis. 'He worked really well with Wrighty, it was a good blend. Alan would link up play really well too.'

Shortly after arriving at Highbury in 1991, Ian Wright said: 'Alan Smith is so easy to play with. He's so unselfish. He'll always create chances, besides scoring himself.'

Former Arsenal midfielder Brian Marwood is similarly effusive in his praise of Smith: 'He had great, natural instincts as a striker; not just his ability to find the net but where to go, when to make his runs and how to make himself available to team-mates. He made my life incredibly easy

Alan leaves an opponent grounded as he turns and heads for goal.

because he made so many intelligent runs into the box, into space. Not all strikers have that ability. Strikers are invariably judged on the number of goals they score, but there's so much more to forward play than that and Alan possessed all the qualities you would look for in a good, all-round centre forward.'

Prior to the signing of Ian Wright in the autumn of 1991, Alan had been the spearhead of Arsenal's attack for four years. The last of these pre-Wright seasons saw Alan play a major role in a second title success, top-scoring with 22 League goals. It was a total that included a hat-trick in a memorable 3–1 victory over Manchester United at Highbury.

The arrival of Wright the following season, however, saw a change in Alan's role within the team. He would now play much more of his football with his back to goal, linking midfield and attack. Inevitably, Alan's strike rate was affected by his new role, but his contribution to the team

remained immense. He played a full part in the Cup successes of 1993 and, a year later, enjoyed his deserved moment of glory in Copenhagen.

'He didn't have the flair, say, of Paul Merson but Alan was very consistent,' remembers Marwood. 'He was very steady, very intelligent and he made the most of the ability he'd got. He was a cultured player and his disciplinary record was impeccable for a striker who took so much stick. He never retaliated, just got on with his job, and I think he was only booked once in his career. Remarkable.'

However, Marwood also points out that Smith was more than just a target man. 'He had excellent technique and that allowed him that extra yard of space to get his shots in – and he was an excellent finisher, especially with that left foot. He didn't really get the plaudits he deserved, perhaps because he didn't court publicity and just got on with his job but his contribution during his time at Highbury should never be underestimated.'

Sylvain Wiltord FACTFILE

155 Appearances

28 Goals

Born: Neuilly-sur-Marne, France, 10 May 1974
Joined Arsenal from Bordeaux in August 2000

Honours: League Championship 2001/02; FA Cup 2002, 2003
International Honours: 50 France caps; European Championship 2000

Third Place

In most teams, Sylvain Wiltord's pace, trickery and eye for goal would mark him out as a unique talent, but in Arsène Wenger's Arsenal side, the presence of Thierry Henry, Robert Pires, Dennis Bergkamp and Freddie Ljungberg complicates matters.

He arrived at Highbury in August 2000, having enhanced his reputation as a skilful and versatile forward the previous summer when he scored for France in the final of the European Championships against Italy. He opened his scoring account in only his second start, netting in the 2–1 win against Coventry in September. A late-season goal flurry, including a hat-trick against West Ham United, saw the Frenchman reveal his true goalscoring pedigree.

The next two seasons saw Sylvain establish himself as a consistent goalscorer, and his strike rate of a goal roughly every three games remains impressive for a player who divides his time between the wing and centre forward. He is an effervescent character and his energetic demeanour is evident in his committed performances on the pitch.

Despite competing with a host of international stars at Highbury, Sylvain emerged from his tricky first season at Highbury to become a key component in Wenger's forward line. During the 2001/02 'double' season, he proved himself to be a skilful and selfless player who can operate in any of the forward positions. Arguably, most effective in a wide, midfield attacking role, he never lost his eye for goal and he gave Arsène Wenger a timely reminder of his talents as a front line striker in the title decider at Old Trafford in May 2002.

In a predictably tense encounter, Sylvain had sufficient composure to take advantage of a goalscoring opportunity, pouncing to score after Fabien Barthez had been unable to hold a Freddie Ljungberg shot. In that moment, Sylvain Wiltord became an instant Highbury legend.

Wiltord scores the goal that takes the title back to Highb[...]

Frank Stapleton plays a short pass.

The Contenders

Frank Stapleton, 1974–1981
(297 appearances, 108 goals)
Frank arrived at Highbury from his native Dublin as a teenager and made his debut in Bertie Mee's first team as a 19-year-old. He was one of those rare players who combined a high level of technical ability with an equally prodigious work-rate, his serious nature marked him out for a bright future in the game.

Frank continued to work hard once he had broken into the senior side, and his efforts saw him improve from an already impressive base to become a top-class striker. His once average first touch soon became exemplary, while his flicks with head or foot became an outstanding feature of his game. However, the greatest strength of Frank's game was his peerless heading ability.

It was a headed goal that brought Frank his most memorable moment in an Arsenal jersey, when he nodded home in the FA Cup final of 1979 won by Arsenal 3–2. Frank subsequently played in each of the three defeated Cup final teams of the Terry Neill era. In the summer of 1981, though, Manchester United made their move for Frank and the Irishman departed for Old Trafford.

Joe Baker, 1962–1966
(157 appearances, 101 goals)
To those too young to have seen him in full flow, Joe Baker was the Ian Wright of his day. To those who can remember the 1960s, there has only ever been one Joe Baker.

Joe was born in Liverpool but raised in Scotland, and his career was a colourful one, reflecting his larger-than-life demeanour and effervescent character. An impish but astonishingly prolific goalscorer, his strike rate of a goal every one-and-a-half games bears comparison with that of any Arsenal legend.

A skilful footballer who, unlike many centre forwards of the day, was a willing contributor to team-play, Joe was also a fine finisher and devastatingly quick. 'He was the quickest man I've ever known over five yards,' recalls Bob Wilson. 'Joe had pace like Thierry Henry. It would have been a very interesting race to see those two go up against one another. Over a longer distance Henry would win, but over a short distance Joe was like lightning. He was a terrific striker and he scared people with his pace.'

But despite his continuous flow of goals in the Arsenal cause, Joe's four-season stay at Highbury bore no silverware, and he moved on to Nottingham Forest in February 1966.

Ian Wright FACTFILE

221
Appearances

128
Goals

Born: Woolwich, London,
3 November 1963
Joined Arsenal from Crystal Palace in
September 1991

Honours: League Championship
1997/98; FA Cup 1993; Coca-Cola Cup 1993
International Honours: 33 England caps

'If he didn't score for six games, he'd believe wholeheartedly that he would **score in the seventh.**'

Paul Davis pays tribute to Wright's self-belief

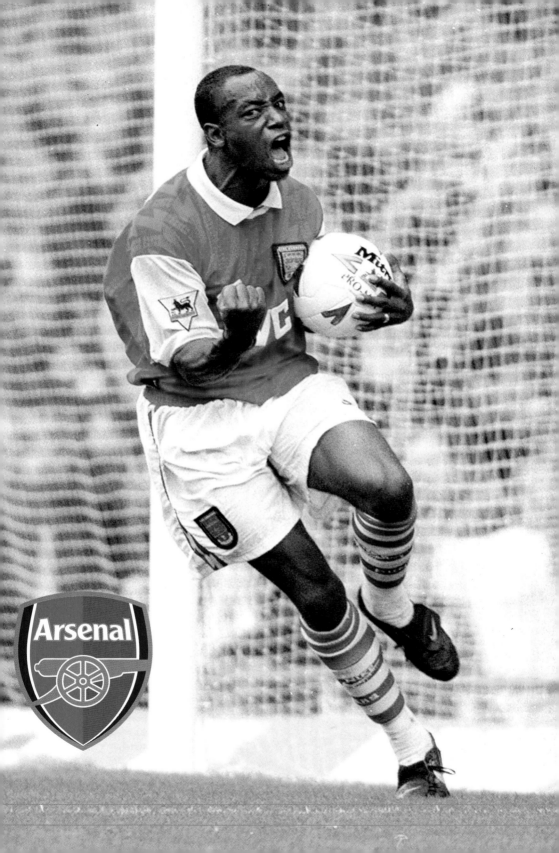

The Ian Wright story demonstrates the truth of the old adage 'If at first you don't succeed, try, try again.' With a swagger and a smile, Wright broke Arsenal goalscoring records galore, while his youthful exuberance left others breathless just watching him. His energy and enthusiasm on the field were matched only by his effervescence off it as he extracted every ounce of enjoyment from a career that had begun with a series of painful rebuffs.

Having suffered the rejection of being released by both Millwall and Brighton, Ian began his senior career in non-League football with Greenwich Borough before making the breakthrough into the professional game with Crystal Palace in 1985. By then he was aged 21, and further setbacks still lay in store in the shape of two broken legs. However, the irrepressible Londoner remained unwavering in his belief that he had the ability and character to make it at the very top of his profession. In 1991 he got his chance when George Graham added him to the Arsenal squad.

Wright could barely contain his excitement after completing his big move across London. 'It was a great move for me, because Arsenal is the club to play for,' explained the England striker. 'If it were just about money, I had a lucrative offer to stay at Palace. I could have gone up north too. But I wanted to play for Arsenal. The challenge should stimulate me. I want to better myself. That should be good for me and Arsenal. I went to the FA Cup final with Palace... At Arsenal we're expected to achieve something like that every season.'

Wright made a flying start to his Arsenal career: a goal in his first game, against Leicester in the League Cup, was followed by a hat-trick against Southampton on his League debut. Settling in had not been a problem, and Tony Adams confirmed: 'Ian Wright has made a fabulous start, and I don't think many teams will fancy meeting our attack.' The new man would partner Alan Smith – a player who had been the First Division's top scorer for two of the previous three seasons.

His character was phenomenal. The only other player I've seen with similar levels of confidence and boisterousness is Paul Gascoigne.

Paul Davis

Ian closes in on goal and Cliff Bastin's record, too.

Ian's first two games were away from home, but his Highbury debut was no less exciting. He scored in a 3–2 League win against London rivals Chelsea and, three days later, found the net again in the second-leg League Cup victory against Leicester. Having begun his Arsenal career with 14 goals from 12 games, he ended the season with another hat-trick against Southampton to take his League tally to 24 in 30 appearances.

Wright had certainly made an immediate impact on the field, and he made a lasting impression on his team-mates off it. Paul Davis recalls: 'His character was phenomenal. The only other player I've seen with similar levels of confidence and boisterousness is Paul Gascoigne. Ian's personality was also infectious. Nothing ever got to him. If he didn't score for six games, he'd believe wholeheartedly that he would score in the seventh. He had such belief.

'As a midfielder Ian was an ideal striker to have in front of you, but if you didn't play the pass he wanted he'd let you know, although he did it in such a way that it wasn't nasty – he just wanted to do well for himself and for the team. He was a great character to have around. It's always good to have somebody like that in your squad or in your team. But with Ian it was the combination of the fact that he has an infectious personality and that he was an outstanding player.'

Former Arsenal striker Alan Smith agrees: 'He is definitely the best goalscorer I have played with. Gary Lineker was an unbelievable player and had a better record for England, but in terms of snapping up half chances there was nobody better than Ian.' The statistics bear that out. But, despite finishing the preceding season as the country's leading scorer with 24 League goals, one ahead of Gary

Ian shows his delight at scoring in the 1993 FA Cup final.

He is definitely the best goalscorer I have played with. In terms of snapping up half chances there was nobody better than Ian.

Alan Smith

Lineker, he was overlooked by England for the 1992 European Championships. The setback merely spurred him on; he hit another 30 goals in all competitions the following season as Arsenal beat Sheffield Wednesday in both the League and the FA Cup finals, with Ian scoring in the replay of the latter.

Soon, Wright began adding records to his medals. He became the fastest Arsenal player to reach 100 goals for the Club, beating Ted Drake's 40-year-old record. Another 30-plus haul in the 1993/94 season underlined his consistency, although the climax to the season was to prove bittersweet for Ian. Having been booked in the semi-final triumph over Paris St Germain and subsequently suspended, he could only watch as Arsenal claimed the European Cup Winners' Cup after a 1–0 win against Parma. But he had more than played his part in getting Arsenal to the final, scoring in the away leg against PSG and contributing four goals in total during the campaign.

After adding another 30 League and Cup goals to his collection during the 1994/95 season, Wright at last got the chance to play in a European final as Arsenal made it all the way once more in the Cup Winners' Cup. His contribution had been to score in every leg of the competition, including crucial goals against Sampdoria in both legs of a semi-final which Arsenal won, dramatically, on penalties. No one was more worthy of a winners' medal than Ian, but he could not maintain his goalscoring run in the final against Real Zaragoza.

In the season following the arrival of Bruce Rioch as manager, Wright managed 23 goals in all competitions, including seven in the League Cup as Arsenal reached the semi-finals before clinching a UEFA Cup spot. By now he had established a promising and exciting understanding with one of Rioch's signings, Dennis Bergkamp. He stayed on for two more years under Arsène Wenger, departing with a League Championship winners' medal in 1998 – and the title of Arsenal's greatest ever goalscorer, having taken his tally to 185 goals in 287 appearances, breaking Cliff Bastin's record with a hat-trick against Bolton on 13 September 1997.

On joining West Ham in the summer of 1998 Wright reflected on his Arsenal career: 'When you consider that I came into football at a late age but have still managed to pick up every domestic honour in the game you cannot be greedy. Some people can play for 15 years and never win a thing, so I've got to be pleased with all that I've achieved.'

The key to his dynamic game, throughout his Arsenal career, had always been superb movement, an uncanny speed of thought and the supreme ability to score wonder goals seemingly out of nothing. His timing was impeccable too; on the

An emotional Wrighty celebrates his Cup final goal against Sheffield Wednesday.

Some people can play for 15 years and never win a thing, so I've got to be pleased with all that I've achieved.

Ian Wright

last day of the 1991/92 season, his first at the Club, he needed a hat-trick to win the Golden Boot. And he did just that in a 5–1 win against Southampton, on the final day of the North Bank's existence.

Ian carried on playing with his characteristic enthusiasm and passion right through his career, ending with Burnley, whom he helped to win promotion back to the First Division after spells with West Ham, Nottingham Forest and Celtic. For his services to football, Wright was awarded the MBE in 2000 and he admits that receiving his award from the Queen was the most 'humbling and nerve-wracking experience' of his life. Having decided to end his career he added: 'It was the right time for me to retire. I could never emulate the success I had with Arsenal – it was unbelievable for me.'

At Highbury, though, Wright continues to have an impact, notably in the development of Thierry Henry, the man tipped to claim Ian's Arsenal goalscoring record one day. Henry has drawn inspiration from the player he replaced as the Club's number one marksman. In the summer of 2000, at the end of his first season at Arsenal, Henry recalled a conversation with experienced campaigner Martin Keown, who told him to watch carefully how his predecessor hunted goals.

'Martin told me that Ian was not any taller nor faster than I was but still scored many goals,' Henry remembered. 'The next game I scored twice and ever since then I watch the video with his 185 goals any time I can.' Something else Arsenal fans have Ian Wright to thank for.

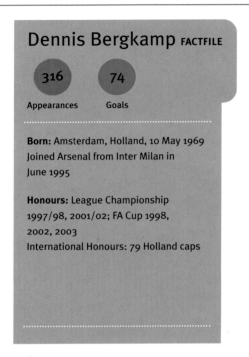

Dennis Bergkamp FACTFILE

316
Appearances

74
Goals

Born: Amsterdam, Holland, 10 May 1969
Joined Arsenal from Inter Milan in
June 1995

Honours: League Championship
1997/98, 2001/02; FA Cup 1998,
2002, 2003
International Honours: 79 Holland caps

> ❛ I don't think there is a better player in the world. He scores goals from outside the box like a midfielder, and he needs fewer touches on the ball than most to score. ❜
>
> Arsène Wenger, 1998

The Runner-up

Dutch legend Marco van Basten, when once asked to put a value on Dennis Bergkamp, said: 'If Ryan Giggs is worth £20 million, Dennis is worth £100 million.' An opinion, perhaps, but nevertheless an indication of the precious gifts which have made Bergkamp an Arsenal hero, and a true Highbury legend.

Dennis began his career at Ajax in the tutelage of Johan Cruyff. In his final three seasons in Amsterdam, Dennis established himself as one of Europe's most coveted and prolific marksmen. A strike rate of 75 goals in 91 games was enough to tempt Inter Milan into a big-money transfer and the Dutchman moved to the San Siro in 1993. However, he failed to produce his best in Italy, perhaps saving it for his time at Highbury, and after two seasons he was eager for a fresh challenge.

So it was that Dennis arrived at Highbury during Bruce Rioch's reign as Arsenal boss, signing along with David Platt in the summer of 1995.

He scored his first goals for Arsenal against Southampton in September 1995, prompting the broadcaster Tom Watt to comment, 'He's made the season for me. I'd pay to watch him train, he's got that much ability.

Bergkamp ended his first season at Highbury with 11 goals in the League and a further five in Cup competitions, a reasonable return first time out – especially for a player who is not an out-and-out striker. There has always been more to Bergkamp than goals, and he is adept at creating them, as Ian Wright would testify after their first 12 months in tandem.

It's not simply the quantity of goals Bergkamp supplies but also their quality. There can be no better proof of that than the fact that in a single month at the start of his third season in an Arsenal shirt he became the first player in 25 years to claim first, second and third place in the BBC's Goal of the Month competition; two of those came from a hat-trick against Leicester City.

The 1997/98 season proved to be the most successful of his career, and everything that is good about Bergkamp was encapsulated in the 3–3 draw at Filbert Street on 27 August, notably his wonderful third goal. It was very similar to the one he was to score at the end of that season in the World Cup against Argentina: impeccable control, first time on the volley, a subtle clip inside the defender and a clinical finish.

During the 'double'-winning season of 1997/98 Dennis was an inspiration, not just with his 22 League and Cup goals, but his all-round contribution and utter class.

Little wonder that he was named PFA Player of the Year and the Football Writers' Player of the Year at the end of a campaign which saw him hit a magnificent peak, even by his own admission. Reflecting on that season, Bergkamp said: 'During the first half of that season, in particular, I played what must be the best football of my career. Everything I tried seemed to work, my body felt fine and everything went for me.'

At the end of that season Arsène Wenger was full of praise for a player he felt was at the peak of his powers: 'I don't think there is a better player in the world. He scores goals from outside the box like a midfielder, and he needs fewer touches on the ball than most to score. Sometimes just one, when others need two or three.'

Bergkamp was used sparingly at the start of the 2001/02 season. However, as the 'double' became an increasing possibility, his influence grew and in the second half of the season the old Dennis was back – as were the League Championship and the FA Cup. Bergkamp reached another career milestone when he notched up his 100th goal for Arsenal in the FA Cup tie against Oxford United on 3 January 2003.

Newcastle's Andy O'Brien looks on in awe as Dennis gets airborne.

John Radford FACTFILE

481 Appearances

149 Goals

Born: Pontefract, Yorkshire, 22 February 1947
Joined Arsenal as an apprentice in October 1962

Honours: League Championship 1970/71; FA Cup 1971; European Fairs Cup 1970
International Honours: 2 England caps

Third Place

John Radford possessed all the qualities required by a centre forward, combining strength and the ability to hold off and turn defenders with subtlety in possession and speed of thought. For a big man he was no slouch either. The year before Arsenal's first League and Cup 'double' in 1971, Radford had already been instrumental in the Club's first ever European triumph, in the 1970 Fairs Cup final against Anderlecht, when he scored one of the three goals which turned round a 1–3 away-leg deficit.

When Arsenal clinched that first 'double' the following year, one of the key factors behind the Club's success was the forward pairing of Radford and rookie striker Ray Kennedy, who would no doubt give huge credit to his more experienced partner for nursing him through his inaugural season. Thrust together as a makeshift partnership only as a result of an injury to John's regular partner Charlie George, Radford and Kennedy were to remain in tandem even after George regained fitness, by which time their partnership was well on the way to a joint total of 46 League and Cup goals.

Kennedy claimed the majority of those goals but the plaudits were shared as Radford's pace, power, mobility and intelligent use of the ball came to the fore. He enjoyed his best ever season of an Arsenal career that spanned 14 years, during which he scored 149 goals from his 481 appearances. Before Ian Wright burst on to the scene, Radford's career tally was second only to that of Cliff Bastin.

Fellow 'double' winner Bob Wilson remains full of admiration for the contribution of Arsenal's prolific front two, and says: 'John was an orthodox forward but for a big guy his mobility was extraordinary. Ray was not as quick as Raddy but he had so much strength that people bounced off him, and he had a wonderful left foot. Ray was brilliant with his back to goal and Raddy was great at spinning his marker.'

At the outset of the 1970s Radford earned international recognition but even though he continued to score goals on a regular basis for Arsenal, his England career was brief, a fact Wilson still fails to understand: 'The skill he had as a centre forward was exceptional and the fact that he only ever won two England caps is amazing.'

John Radford: a tall targetman with excellent touch.

The Contenders

Malcolm MacDonald, 1976–1979
(107 appearances, 42 goals)

Although his Arsenal career was curtailed by a knee injury, Macdonald made sufficient impact to more than justify the 'Supermac' tag he had gained at Newcastle.

The former Fulham and Luton striker became the only England player to score five goals in one match for his country, against Cyprus at Wembley in 1975, and he arrived at Highbury in 1976 with a massive reputation.

There was nothing fancy about Malcolm's style; he was all about pace, power and purpose. When he was in full stride there was little opposition defences could do to halt his progress towards goal, where his finishing was as direct as his approach. For a relatively short striker, standing little more than 5ft 8in, he possessed a prodigious leap which often caught taller defenders unawares.

In his first season at Highbury he top-scored with 29 goals and his next campaign produced 26, including seven in the FA Cup as he powered Arsenal to Wembley. He scored in every round bar the final against Ipswich but, as had been the case five years earlier with Newcastle, left Wembley a loser. Sadly, a year later, injuries forced him to exit football for good at the age of only 29.

'Supermac' fires a shot at goal.

Ted Drake, 1934–1939
(186 appearances, 139 goals)

Ted Drake is regarded by many as Arsenal's greatest ever centre forward. Strong and brave, he led the line for Arsenal with both courage and skill throughout the second half of the 1930s.

Ted arrived at Arsenal in March 1934 as the first major signing of George Allison, the man who had succeeded the great Herbert Chapman as manager a few months earlier. As it turned out, Allison could not have made a more impressive first foray into the transfer market.

Drake was an instant success at Highbury. He scored on his debut in a 3–2 victory at home to Wolves and added six more goals in his next nine matches. His first full season brought an even more impressive strike rate, with Drake netting 12 times in the opening 12 games. Drake's early-season haul already included two hat-tricks, and he repeated the feat against Spurs to become the first Arsenal player to score three times in a match at the Lane.

At the end of his first full season at Arsenal, Drake had scored 42 League goals in 41 games. Allison's judgement had proved astute and Arsenal had successfully defended their League title for a second time.

Drake's most remarkable Drake feat came in December 1935 at Villa Park where the Arsenal centre forward scored all the goals in a 7–1 demolition of Aston Villa. It was an achievement all the more notable since Drake played despite a knee injury that soon required surgery. He would recover in time to play a telling role in the 1936 Cup final win over Sheffield United, scoring the only goal of the game after 76 minutes before collapsing due to the pain in his injured knee.

Drake was also a contributor to Arsenal's final success of the 1930s. His goals were vital to the League triumph of 1938/39, but he will also be remembered for his bravery against Championship rivals Brentford at Griffin Park when he played on despite two broken bones in his wrist and several stitches in his head before eventually being carried off unconscious by coach Tom Whittaker.

Robert Pires FACTFILE

138
Appearances

27
Goals

Born: Reims, France, 29 January 1973
Joined Arsenal from Olympique Marseille
in July 2000

Honours: League Championship
2001/02; FA Cup 2003
International Honours: 54 France caps;
World Cup 1998; European
Championship 2000

'I'm delighted for Robert because he is a wonderful person,
not just a **fantastic footballer**.

He has played a major part in our success this season...'

Arsène Wenger on Pires' Footballer Writers' Association Player of the Year award

If ever evidence were needed that first impressions can be misleading, it was provided in abundance during Robert Pires's first Arsenal season. A high-profile signing from Olympique Marseille and a World Cup winner, Robert arrived at Highbury in the wake of Marc Overmars's move to Barcelona in the summer of 2000 and was greeted by a wave of expectation in London N5.

However, adjusting to a new club, a new style of football and new team-mates is not easy and – just like many of his predecessors from abroad – Robert took his time to settle. However, the 26-year-old Frenchman soon won over any doubters in emphatic style and mutterings from the terraces gave way to outpourings of admiration towards Arsène Wenger's new number seven. By the end of his second season, he was being fêted by everyone from Arsenal fans to the Professional Footballers' Association.

In his first few months as an Arsenal player, Robert had needed to come to terms with not only the frenetic and physical nature of English football but also new team-mates and new tactical ideas. The result was an uncharacteristically cautious Robert Pires. Thankfully, Robert was soon back to his buoyant best, playing the role of midfield creator with the refreshing combination of verve and artistry that would come to be his trademark.

Pires's arrival at Highbury came from a journey that began with his home town club Reims, taking in a six-year spell at Metz before two eventful seasons at Marseille. His first season at the Vélodrome saw him play a major role in a run to the UEFA Cup final and a sustained Championship challenge.

Arsène Wenger wasted little time in registering his interest in a player whom he had tried to sign for Monaco several years before. This time, Arsène would get his man, despite competing interest from Real Madrid. However, with Pires on duty with the France national team at Euro 2000 he would have to be patient. Eventually the deal was concluded on the day after Robert had helped France clinch the European Championship with a 2–1 extra-time victory over Italy.

> I arrived here with a game that wasn't really suited to English football. It was hard, but after five or six months I started to adapt and it has gone better and better since.

Robert Pires

Team-mates and fans alike pay their respect to the midfield maestro.

However, nothing could have prepared Pires for the challenge that awaited him. After the usual rigorous pre-season, the 6ft 1in Frenchman was left to watch from the bench as Arsenal kicked off their campaign with a 1–0 defeat at Sunderland. Wenger had told his new playmaker: 'I'm starting you on the bench today so you can get a feel for the game and what it's like here.' Pires was happy with this, but his contented expression began to disappear as he watched a full-blooded and typically frenetic Premiership match unfold at the Stadium of Light. 'After about 25 minutes I was at a loss,' recalled Pires in his autobiography *Robert Pires Footballeur*, 'I'd never seen such thundering tackling, all studs up with arms flailing – how was I going to make my mark in this type of football?'

The truth was that Robert would have to be patient. Physically tired after a taxing season for club and country and facing a demanding new challenge, he remained a peripheral figure during the first six months of his debut campaign at Highbury. There were occasional foretastes of the kind of sublime skill that would soon become Robert's standard, most memorably in October when he scored his first two goals for Arsenal in away matches against Lazio and West Ham United. However, it was not until mid-January that the Highbury faithful were able to witness a Pires goal at first hand. That strike – a third-minute opener in a 1–1 draw against Chelsea – coincided with a gradual improvement in Robert's form. He would later comment, 'I arrived here with a game that wasn't really suited to English football. And I was probably a little tired after a difficult season at Marseille. It was hard, but after five or six months I started to adapt and it has gone better and better since.'

By the early spring of 2001, the Frenchman was exerting a growing influence on the field, thereby rewarding the faith Arsène Wenger had showed in him earlier in the season. Two goals against Tottenham Hotspur in eight days – one of them the winner in an FA Cup semi-final – did much to further endear Robert to both the Arsenal manager and the Club's fans. By the season's end, his slow start to the campaign had been long forgotten, and with a record of eight goals in 51 appearances he had made a major contribution to the 2000/01 Arsenal campaign.

Arsenal's fans had, by now, come to realize the mercurial Pires's immense talent. Robert had been described as a winger on his arrival, but the label does not do his extensive skills justice. He has pace and the ability to take on opponents, but he is more than just a touchline-hugging wide man. Robert has an

He's a nice guy... I am always pleased to work with players like him, who don't get a big head, who say hello to everyone in the morning, and don't let success change them.

Former Metz manager Joel Muller

Robert lifts the ball over the keeper at Villa Park in March 2002.

assured touch in both feet, plays with vision and scores his share of goals too, however, what sets him apart from other attacking midfielders, is his speed of thought. There is no erring, no hesitation. When Robert receives the ball, he knows instantly what he is going to do with it, and unlike many creative players he is happy to play one- and two-touch football when the need arises. Thierry Henry would be the first to applaud his compatriot's ability to pick an early pass, as he has regularly been the beneficiary of his probing deliveries from midfield.

Expectation was high for Robert and his team-mates ahead of the 2001/02 season and, just like the previous campaign, it kicked off with an awkward trip to the North-East. Arsenal's opponents were Middlesbrough, and this time Arsène Wenger had no hesitation in playing Pires from the start. The World Cup-winning midfielder did not disappoint, scoring a penalty and playing a full part in a 4–0 win for the visitors. It was the perfect start.

Whether playing centrally or on the left or right, Robert maintained a consistently high standard, creating and scoring goals with impressive regularity. By mid-season Arsenal were making good progress in the Champions League and topped the Premiership table, and Pires's form was a major factor in this success. The Frenchman's combination play with Henry, Freddie Ljungberg and Sylvain Wiltord was a joy to behold, frequently cutting swathes through opposing defences with an irresistible blend of pace and skill.

Robert himself scored his 12th goal of the season with a sublime finish against Aston Villa at Villa Park on 17 March. With Villa's George Boateng in close attendance, he received the ball on the left touchline, drew a challenge from the Dutchman before flicking it over his head and moving inside to dispatch an inch-perfect lob over Peter Schmeichel who watched helplessly on his six-yard line. Robert's next goal came courtesy of a curling shot in the FA Cup sixth-round replay

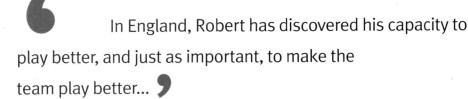

'In England, Robert has discovered his capacity to play better, and just as important, to make the team play better...'

Tiburce Darrou – the Fitness Trainer who helped Robert recover from ligament damage

against Newcastle at Highbury; however, it would be quickly forgotten, as within 25 minutes of scoring, the joy of celebration was replaced by the agony of injury.

Robert had tried to hurdle a challenge from Newcastle's Nicos Dabizas but had fallen awkwardly and twisted his knee. Initially, at least, he was optimistic about the prognosis, believing he would be out for just a few weeks, but a specialist soon gave a more depressing verdict. Robert had damaged the cruciate ligament in his right knee and his season was over. With Arsenal challenging for the 'double' and France looking to defend the World Cup, Pires had been hoping for a tumultuous conclusion to an already exciting season. Instead, he faced surgery followed by a gruelling rehabilitation programme that would require dedication and a summer of hard work. He would meet the challenge head on.

In the meantime, there was no shortage of tributes for Pires. The Football Writers' association voted him their Player of the Year, while his own team-mates bowed down to him with a 'We're not worthy' gesture as they celebrated the Premiership title in May 2002. Robert was a worthy recipient of all the acclaim that came his way and his contribution to the 2001/02 'double' season was indisputably significant.

However, with his ligament repaired and the medals and awards safely ensconced in the trophy cabinet, Robert was left to travel the lonely road back to fitness during the summer of 2003 while his compatriots jetted off to the Far East and the World Cup finals.

Robert's rehab was carried out in the south of France and he has since confessed that it was the hardest he had ever trained. 'Each day began with a 40-kilometre bike ride and a session in the gym before lunch... There were times when it was really hard,' recalled the midfielder. 'I tried not to complain. It wasn't a serious injury, not in the context of life.'

With the hard work done, Robert returned to London at the beginning of September 2002 and spent a month working on the training pitch to improve his football-related fitness. On 22 October Arsène Wenger recalled Robert to first-team duty with a substitute appearance against Auxerre. 'I thought my heart was going to cave in,' Pires later confessed. 'I wanted to run all over the place.'

Speaking shortly after his return to fitness, Robert explained his ambitions for the remainder of the 2002/03 season: 'To find my game. To find my technique. To win my place back on the team. To win my place back on the French team...

I'm not going to rush into anything. There is another seven months to run in the Championship. I'm not worried. I know eventually it will come back but it's not going to happen all at once.' However, patience would not be required on this occasion. By November Robert was once more a regular in Arsenal's first team and a mid-season run of seven goals in ten Premiership starts left nobody in any doubt that he was back. His form remained impressive throughout the remainder of the season and a hat-trick against Southampton in Arsenal's penultimate Premiership fixture took his goal tally to 14 in 20 starts. However, the best was saved for last, and it was fitting that Robert – who had missed the 2002 FA Cup final through injury – should score the only goal in the Cup final win against Southampton at the Millennium Stadium.

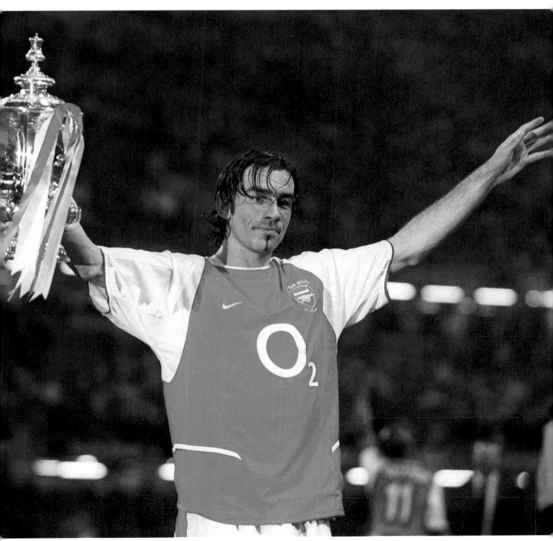

Another vital goal and another trophy – Robert with the 2003 FA Cup.

Marc Overmars FACTFILE

100
Appearances

25
Goals

Born: Emst, Holland, 29 March 1973
Joined Arsenal from Ajax in July 1997

Honours: League Championship
1997/98; FA Cup 1998
International Honours: 74 Holland caps

> ❛ He was upset at the rumours he was not fit and that he could never play to his true ability again. That was a good sign for me, a hurt player. He had something to prove. ❜

Arsène Wenger on his decision to sign Marc Overmars

The Runner-up

During his time at Arsenal, Marc Overmars had tormented the country's defenders, leaving most in his trail as he jetted towards goal. At full speed, he was uncatchable and his forays forward frequently led to goals, many scored by Marc himself.

The former Ajax forward had arrived at Highbury in 1997. He came with a big reputation, having established an international profile with a succession of high-class performances for Holland. However, Marc had only recently recovered from a cruciate ligament injury and nobody could be sure he would be able to regain his pre-injury form.

Arsène Wenger was confident he was buying a player who was both fit enough and mentally strong enough to withstand the rigours of the Premiership. 'When I did my homework on him I discovered he was upset at the rumours he was not fit and that he could never play to his true ability again. That was a good sign for me, a hurt player. He had something to prove.'

He would make his point in emphatic style, helping his new team to the League and FA Cup 'double' in his first season at Arsenal and

contributing 14 goals in the process. It was a total that made Marc the Club's second-top scorer behind his compatriot Dennis Bergkamp. The Dutch duo proved a devastating combination, with Bergkamp's ability to put measured passes into space proving the perfect complement to Overmars's pace and direct running.

He was a skilful ball player – you do not wear the number eleven jerseys of Ajax, Arsenal and Holland unless you have a trick or two – Marc's style was refreshingly straightforward and direct. There were no unnecessary embellishments and no showboating. Instead, Marc would control the ball and manoeuvre himself to face goal as quickly as possible before racing towards his target. The cross-shot arrowed across the goalkeeper and usually delivered low and hard was a favourite and profitable weapon. Marc was also quick to break forward when the ball was on the right wing, and he was frequently on hand to finish moves with an adroit touch in the penalty area.

The undoubted highlights of Marc's first season at Highbury came with important goals against Manchester United and Newcastle United, each of which was critical to the story of Arsenal's second 'double' season. The goal against Alex Ferguson's team at Old Trafford in March was of huge

Marc opens the scoring for Arsenal in the 1998 Cup final at Wembley.

significance as it earned Arsenal a 1–0 victory and gave them hope as they mounted an improbable title challenge. Wenger's team had been nine points behind United, but when Marc skipped clear of the home defence to collect Nicolas Anelka's flick and dispatch the ball between Peter Schmeichel's legs the Championship race was blown wide open. Two months later with the Premiership crown secured, Marc took centre stage in the FA Cup final victory over Newcastle at Wembley. The Dutchman once more opened the scoring, bursting clear of his marker to collect Emmanuel Petit's pass and slip the ball between Shay Given's legs.

For the next two seasons, Marc continued to frighten Premiership defences but neither he nor Arsenal managed to reclaim the heights of that memorable 'double' campaign of 1997/98. One thing, however, that should be made clear is that the Dutch winger was a committed and wholehearted performer who always gave of his best. His commitment was never more clearly illustrated than in February 1998 when he played in an FA Cup tie against Crystal Palace despite returning from international duty in the United States with Holland only on the morning of the game. Arsène Wenger was clearly delighted at the midfielder's efforts and declared after the game: 'It was a big surprise that we could have him playing at all. Last night he was in America playing for Holland but he was able to catch a flight to Paris and was back in London this morning.'

In the summer of 2000, however, Marc was unable to resist the temptation offered by a new challenge at Barcelona and he departed for the Nou Camp. So, how good a player was Marc Overmars for Arsenal? Well, it took Robert Pires to replace him and that probably tells the story.

Paul Merson FACTFILE

327 Appearances

78 Goals

Born: Brent, London, 20 March 1968
Joined Arsenal as an apprentice in
July 1984

Honours: League Championship
1988/89, 1990/91; FA Cup 1993;
League Cup 1993; European Cup
Winners' Cup 1994
International Honours: 21 England caps

Third Place

Paul Merson is a footballer who played the game for Arsenal with a freedom of spirit and creative verve that have become all too rare. To his credit, the likeable Londoner has always retained his passion for the game and for entertaining paying supporters, and he remains a hugely popular figure with Arsenal fans.

Paul joined the Gunners in 1985 and a year later was a member of the Club's FA Youth Cup-winning team that triumphed 6–1 over Doncaster Rovers. He made his first-team debut in November 1986 with George Graham commenting: 'He's a very intelligent young player who makes some excellent runs off the ball.' Brian Marwood was among Paul's team-mates during the early years and remembers that the youngster was 'earmarked for great things from an early age', adding: 'But obviously success as a player is not just about ability and in Paul's case it was as much about keeping his feet on the ground, remaining focused and, generally, being a good pro.'

The roguish smile never far from his face, Merson's progress on the pitch was unrelenting in the late 1980s and early 1990s. Championship

medals in 1988/89 and 1990/91 were duly collected, along with the PFA Young Player of the Year award (also in 1989) and a full England call-up in 1992.

Paul's early progress on the pitch was aided by his versatility, and George Graham deployed him in a variety of midfield and attacking roles, though he was never happier than when afforded a free role behind the main striker, allowing him to move from wing to wing and utilize the space in between the opposing team's defence and midfield.

In the autumn of 1996 Merson earned an England recall and was once more enjoying his football following Arsène Wenger's appointment as Arsenal manager. However, in the summer of 1997 his magnificent Arsenal career came to an end when he joined Middlesbrough.

Merson in full flow for the Gunners.

Limps sinks to his knees in celebration.

The Contenders

Anders Limpar, 1990–1994
(96 appearances, 20 goals)
Anders Limpar's presence at Highbury during George Graham's reign represents something of a curiosity. A winger who liked to go forward but loathed to go back, he was an artist, a maverick; the kind of player wholly at odds with Graham's generally cautious approach to the game.

But Arsenal fans were extremely grateful that their manager had decided to sign Limpar from Italian side Cremonese in the summer of 1990. The Swede proved an instant hit, adding much-needed variety to the side's attack with his marauding raids down the left flank.

Anders could be extravagant with tricks and feints, but his greatest asset was a venomous shot, which he demonstrated to devastating effect throughout his first season. He scored 11 times in 34 appearances in helping his new club to the League Championship. However, perhaps his most memorable strike came the following season when he struck a 50-yard lob over Liverpool keeper Mike Hooper at Highbury in April 1992.

Alas, he was to spend much of the next season on the bench, and he played his last game for the Club in a 4–0 victory over Southampton at the Dell on 19 March 1994.

Cliff Bastin, 1929–1946
(402 appearances, 182 goals)
Cliff Bastin was one of the true stars of Arsenal's great team of the 1930s. Until 1997, when Ian Wright surpassed his feat, he was the Club's record scorer. However, what is most remarkable about Bastin's achievement is that he scored his goals from the wing rather than as a centre forward. Few wide men in the history of English football can boast a more prolific strike rate than Cliff.

Herbert Chapman had brought the 17-year-old Bastin to Highbury from Exeter in 1929, and within months he was an Arsenal regular on the left wing. At the age of just 18 years and one month, Bastin was the youngest player to appear in an FA Cup final, although he was clearly not overawed by the occasion and after 16 minutes his pass led to Arsenal's opening goal in a 2–0 win.

FA Cup final success brought a rewarding end to Bastin's first season as a Gunner. The Devon-born winger would, however, enjoy many more highlights during a glittering Highbury career. By the age of 21 he had won every honour in English soccer and by the time he retired shortly after the war, he had made 402 appearances in all competitions, scoring 182 goals.

Tom Whittaker would explain that Bastin was blessed by an inner calm, commenting: 'Coupled with his sincerity and loyalty to all his bosses, he had a trait few of us are blessed with – that is, he had an ice-cold temperament.'

Cliff's temperament was, no doubt, a key factor in his goalscoring. His ability to find the net soon became legendary, as did his left wing combination with Alex James. Bastin, however, did not always understand the thick Scots accent of his colleague and lightheartedly commented: 'Alex and I may have developed a well-nigh perfect understanding on the field, but off it I always found him a trifle incomprehensible.'

In 1932/33, Cliff scored 33 League goals in helping the Gunners to the Championship. He would contribute significantly to the League successes in each of the next two seasons, before earning his last silverware when George Allison's team won the title again in 1937/38.

Arsène Wenger FACTFILE

259
League games
in charge

151
League
games won

Born: Strasbourg, France, 1949
Joined Arsenal as manager from Nagoya
Grampus Eight in September 1996
Managerial reign: 1996–present

Honours: League Championship
1997/98, 2001/02; FA Cup 1998, 2002,
2003; League Managers' Association
Manager of the Year 1997/98,
Barclaycard Manager of the Year 2001/02

'He's a special guy. He has **transformed** the Club

from start to finish: his training ground methods, his dietary controls

and the way he's extended players' careers. He's made average players

good, good players very good and very good players

world class'

David Dein

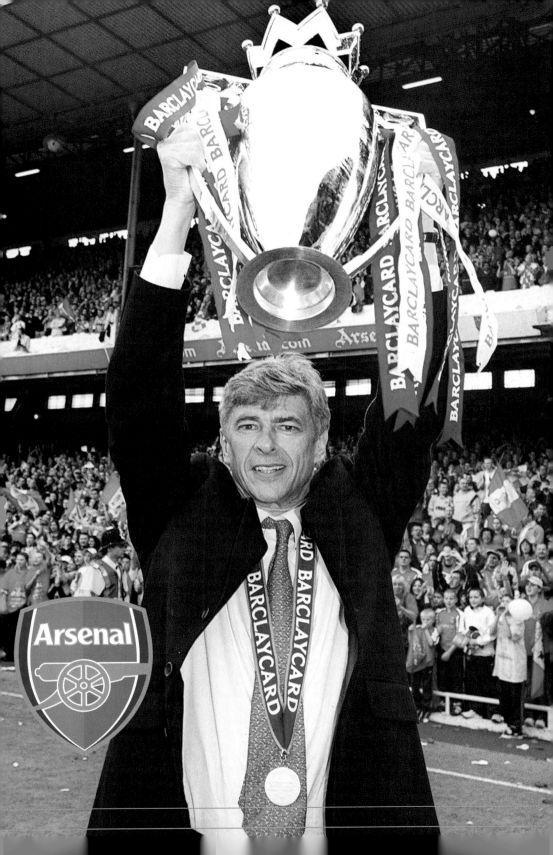

When, back in August 1996, stories began to circulate that Arsenal's new manager was to be a French coach called Arsène Wenger, Highbury was hardly overwhelmed with excitement. Most supporters had never heard of Wenger and, while some well-read fans pretended to be aware of the coaching credentials of a man who was reported to be 'well respected within the game', few genuinely knew anything about him.

Seven years on, of course, Arsène is rather better known within English football, and the success he has brought to Arsenal has made him the emphatic choice as manager of the team selected by supporters in the poll for this book.

Whatever the doubters may have thought in 1996, it quickly became clear that Arsenal had done their homework on a man who had also been thinking over an offer to become the FA's technical director. His CV was impressive: having built his reputation as an intelligent and innovative coach at Nancy, Arsène had taken Monaco to the French Championship before taking charge at Nagoya Grampus Eight in the Japanese J-League.

Within football circles, Arsenal's capture of the 46-year-old Frenchman was recognized as something of a coup. It also became evident that Arsène's knowledge of French football was undimmed by his spell in Japan. Patrick Vieira and Remi Garde were both signed on the new manager's advice in the summer of 1996. What is often overlooked, however, is that Arsène also made a careful assessment of the players and staff he had inherited from his predecessor Bruce Rioch. There was no wholesale change, no purge and no prejudice. Change was gradual and decisions were made pragmatically as Arsène attempted to inject modern, continental methods and ideas without undermining the qualities and expertise of those already at the Club. It was this approach that ensured the continued service of men like Pat Rice and Bob Wilson, and most notably the retention of the defensive five that had served the Club so well since the late 1980s.

To have achieved what he has done is the most extraordinary feat... for a London club to win the Championship is an achievement in itself.

Bob Wilson gives his verdict on Arsène's record of two 'doubles' in five seasons

Wilson explains, 'Arsène has admitted that he never thought he'd have a back four with an average age of 35 but he allowed them to prove a point to him. He knew the importance of those players.'

Arsène's subtle style of management saw him focus clearly on the areas of his team that were weak and on players who were underperforming, while leaving the back four and other areas alone. It's a simple but effective philosophy that invites reference to the cliché 'if it's not broken don't fix it'. As Robert Pires confirms: 'He'll talk to you a lot when you first join the Club, or whenever he feels you're off your game... [but] when he senses you're at ease, he'll simply let you be.'

In fact, simplicity is behind much of Arsène's approach to management. Instructions are kept to a minimum, tactics are uncomplicated and responsibilities are clearly communicated. Everything is succinct, everything is focused.

Arsène told Arsenal's official magazine: 'I have never been the type to change a system if a couple of results didn't go your way... In my early days I looked for a coherent, adaptable system and tried to get my team used to that. I was aware that there was no one ideal system, but I knew that a team that played a system as well as they can, have a chance, but in every system there are weaknesses.'

However, there were few weaknesses in Arsène's 4–4–2 formation during his first full season in charge at Highbury. Once he had reinforced his team with the likes of Marc Overmars, Emmanuel Petit and Gilles Grimandi, Arsenal swept to the League and FA Cup 'double' in 1997/98, thus emulating the achievement of Bertie Mee's famed team of 1970/71. It was also notable that among the many stars of the second 'double' was a young player whom Arsène had acquired from Paris St Germain the previous spring. Teenage striker Nicolas Anelka scored nine League and Cup goals that season. Brought to the Club as a promising 18-year-old for a modest fee he emerged as a truly world-class forward before transferring for a record sum to Real Madrid in 1999.

Bob Wilson, who has worked alongside Arsène as Arsenal's goalkeeping coach, is in no doubt about the magnitude of his achievements. 'What you must understand about Arsène Wenger is that he's trying to compete with the richest club in the world, a club that has twice the amount of spectators for every game and with three times the commercial return as Arsenal,' says Wilson. 'For him to achieve what he has done is the most extraordinary feat for a club that is not in the same financial bracket as Manchester United. Nobody seems to recognize his achievements. For a London club to win the Championship is an achievement in itself. '

In his autobiography *Robert Pires Footballeur* Pires gives further insight into Arsène's unique style of management. 'His pre-match talk lasts seven minutes – any longer and he reckons it would be counter-productive... it's all very compressed and to the point. For him, football has to be a game everyone can understand.'

Arsène's concise team talks are delivered with characteristic calm. However, despite his unflustered demeanour, the Arsenal manager is as passionate about the game as any Premiership manager.

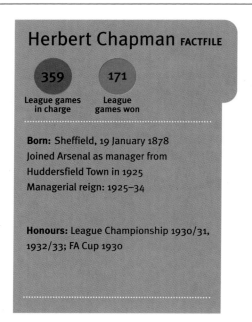

Herbert Chapman FACTFILE

359 League games in charge

171 League games won

Born: Sheffield, 19 January 1878
Joined Arsenal as manager from Huddersfield Town in 1925
Managerial reign: 1925–34

Honours: League Championship 1930/31, 1932/33; FA Cup 1930

> In the dressing room nobody had anything to say, yet each of us knew what [the others] were thinking. Herbert had been loved by us all.

Cliff Bastin, recalling the emotional scene in the Arsenal dressing-room shortly after Chapman's death in 1934

The Contenders

Yorkshireman Herbert Chapman was unquestionably the most successful manager of the inter-war years, and as the poll for this book has proved, his achievements have not been forgotten by Arsenal fans. In the 1930s Chapman's team swept all before them, dominating English football. Unfortunately Herbert would not live to witness all of his team's successes, but the side he built claimed five League Championships and two FA Cups during a golden era at Highbury. Fittingly his contribution to the Arsenal story was honoured by the Club who commissioned a bronze bust in his likeness that sits in pride of place amid the marble halls of N5.

Chapman arrived at Highbury in 1925, taking over a club that was ambitious but which had no track record for success, only a reputation for underachievement. He quickly set about improving the Arsenal playing staff with a succession of notable signings. First, and perhaps most significantly, he brought back legendary inside forward Charlie Buchan who had been a reserve team player for the Club 16 years earlier. Chapman wanted a leader on the pitch, a player of quality and experience who would direct his midfield and boost morale. Buchan's return proved a huge success and soon he was joined by a host of other top-class players. By 1927 Chapman had also signed centre forward Jack Lambert, Herbert Roberts from Oswestry, Kettering's left back Eddie Hapgood, Bolton's England international inside forward David Jack, Scot Alex James from Preston North End and a 16-year-old winger, Cliff 'Boy' Bastin from Exeter.

Chapman also collaborated with Buchan to devise a new tactical system that proved instrumental in Arsenal's successes of the 1930s. The 'WM' formation or third back game was intended to counter a change in the offside law that made life easier for the attacking team. Herbie Roberts was deployed as the 'third back' or stopper and his no-nonsense defending proved a revelation, while Alex James took over the pivotal role in midfield in the new system.

In 1930 Chapman led Arsenal to their first major honour when his team triumphed over Huddersfield Town in the 'Graf Zeppelin Cup final'. The Gunners won 2–0 with the giant Zeppelin airship making the occasion all the more memorable with a flight over Wembley mid-match, briefly casting the great stadium in shadow.

A year later Arsenal won the League Championship for the first time in the Club's history, doing so with a record points total of 66 and scoring 127 goals to become the first southern club to win the trophy. They were runners-up in both the League and Cup in 1932, but second place wasn't good enough for Chapman and the next two seasons they were crowned Champions.

However, on 6 January 1934 the affable Yorkshireman died unexpectedly with his team en route to their third League triumph. The Arsenal manager had caught a heavy cold while on scouting missions in Bury and Sheffield, and had ignored doctor's advice to stay at home and rest. Instead he went to watch Arsenal's third team on a bitterly cold day in Guildford and his cold turned into pneumonia. Thirty-six hours later he was dead.

Within hours, Arsenal's players were arriving at Highbury for a vital match against Sheffield Wednesday. Inside forward Cliff Bastin later recalled: 'As I approached the ground, the newspaper sellers were shouting out the news of Chapman's death. It seemed just too bad to be true. In the dressing room nobody had anything to say, yet each of us knew what [the others] were thinking. Herbert had been loved by us all.'

George Allison took over as Arsenal manager and completed the job that Chapman had started, leading the team to back-to-back Championships in 1933/34 and 1934/35 and the FA Cup in 1936.

Herbert Chapman was more than a club manager. He was also a football pioneer whose influence extended beyond tactics, team management and training. Chapman's ideas and innovations were manifold, and much of his work is still evident in the modern game. He was, of course, the man who instigated the first numbered shirts, which were worn by Arsenal despite initial reticence on the part of the FA. He was also instrumental in achieving floodlit football, and he proposed the ten-yard semi-circle a full decade before it was finally adopted. Similarly, he was a keen advocate of the single England manager rather than a selection committee – an idea that wasn't adopted until after the Second World War. Such was his persuasive skill and persistence that in 1932 he even managed to convince London Electric Railway (who ran the Piccadilly Line) to change the name of Gillespie Road tube station to 'Arsenal'. It is small wonder that his bust – by famous sculptor Jacob Epstein – sits in the entrance hall of the East Stand to survey all he helped create.

Herbert Chapman: legendary Arsenal manager of the 1930s.

George Graham FACTFILE

350 — League games in charge

162 — League games won

Born: Coatbridge, Scotland, 30 November 1944

Joined Arsenal as manager from Millwall in 1986

Managerial reign: 1986–95

Honours: League Championship 1988/89, 1990/91; FA Cup 1993; League Cup 1987, 1993; European Cup Winners' Cup 1994

The Contenders

As a player George Graham could appear languid, even disinterested, but as a manager he had a reputation for rigour and discipline that made a mockery of the nickname, 'Stroller', he had earned during his days as a goalscoring midfielder. George, who had won the 'double' as a player at Highbury in 1970/71, cut his managerial teeth at Millwall before taking over at Arsenal in 1986.

He inherited a team that had been woefully inconsistent for several seasons and had won nothing since the 1979 Cup final. A mixture of young emergent stars, like Rocastle, Adams and Quinn, and experienced players, such as Woodcock, Mariner and Sansom, and it soon became clear that Graham would need to rebuild his team. In the meantime, the Scotsman did at least give Arsenal fans something to cheer about in his first full season in charge, leading the Club to a League Cup final win over Liverpool.

The following season it became clear exactly which area of his team George was targeting for most urgent reinforcement. Defence would become the bedrock on which he built his side, and he recruited both Nigel Winterburn and Lee Dixon

during 1987/88. A second successive League Cup final appearance followed but George's men were defensively vulnerable and conceded three times in losing to Luton Town at Wembley.

George's reaction was predictable but effective. Stoke centre half Steve Bould duly arrived to join his former club-mate, Dixon, and so the legendary back four of the 1980s and 1990s was complete. The quartet of Dixon, Winterburn, Adams and Bould would become the greatest defence in the Club's history, providing stoical service for a decade.

Their manager was, however, not satisfied with merely assembling the right personnel, he also went to great lengths to make sure that his defence operated as an effective unit by extensive work on the training ground. Brian Marwood recalls vividly the hours George spent with his defenders in practice: 'George worked relentlessly with them on the training field in his quest to achieve perfection. And you've have to say, it wasn't far off that.'

With his defence organized and his midfield boosted by the presence of such enterprising talent as Marwood, Davis, Rocastle and Thomas, George completed his team-building by signing Leicester's Alan Smith. The jigsaw came together ahead of the 1988/89 season and Arsenal clinched their first League Championship for 18 years in dramatic fashion with a 2–0 victory at Anfield on the final day of the season.

Graham would take even more pride from the style of his team's second Championship success, which came two years after the first. Arsenal, whose defence had been further reinforced by the arrival of David Seaman in goal, conceded just 18 goals all season and lost only one League game.

In 1991 came arguably George's most popular signing – Ian Wright. Arsenal now had a player with the goalscoring potenial and panache to grace any team. Two years later, with Wright as their talisman, George's team completed a unique domestic Cup 'double', beating Sheffield Wednesday in both finals. A year later came European success in the Cup Winners' Cup against Parma, but the undoubted pinnacle of George's nine-year Highbury reign, however, was the winning of that 1990/91 Championship.

THE GREAT GOALS

Although the purveyors of football cliché may tell us that it 'doesn't matter how they come', we all know that some goals are worthy of special status. A goal may be technically remarkable, for example Dennis Bergkamp's unforgettable turn and shot against Newcastle in 2002, or it may be great due to its context, witness Charlie George's unforgettable finish in the 1971 FA Cup final. Of course, deciding whether a goal is great is a matter of subjective judgement, something that was put to the test in the poll for this book.

When the votes had been counted Arsenal's greatest goals ranked in the following order:

1. Michael Thomas v Liverpool
at Anfield, Division One, 26 May 1989
2. Dennis Bergkamp v Newcastle
at St James' Park, FA Barclaycard Premiership, 2 March 2002
3. Tony Adams v Everton
at Highbury, FA Carling Premiership, 3 May 1998
4. Charlie George v Liverpool
at Wembley Stadium, FA Cup final, 8 May 1971
5. Alan Sunderland v Manchester United
at Wembley Stadium, FA Cup final, 12 May 1979

Thomas lifts the ball over Grobbelaar to score the 'greatest goal' in Arsenal's history.

WINNER

Michael Thomas v Liverpool
at Anfield, Division One, 26 May 1989

It is hard to imagine that a better timed or more dramatic goal will ever be scored in English football than the one that clinched the League Championship for Arsenal in May 1989. In its execution Michael Thomas's decisive strike was not especially remarkable but placed in context it was a truly spectacular goal.

It is a night that Paul Davis remembers well. 'Before the game George Graham talked us through the situation, he told us how the game would unfold. He said, "The first half will be tight, but we'll score the first goal, they'll wobble and we'll get the second." And that's exactly what happened.'

Alan Smith was the man who scored the first goal, but it was left to Michael Thomas, a homegrown player and a Londoner to score the tumultuous second.

Thomas recalls the goal singled out by Arsenal supporters as their most memorable of all: 'I'd had a chance a few minutes before when Kevin Richardson had played the ball through to me, but I snatched at the ball and dragged it wide. Maybe a lot of people thought that our chance had gone, but I didn't. I just had a funny feeling that I would get another chance to redeem myself and, sure enough, I did.

'The game itself is a bit of a blur, it just seemed to fly by, like a Cup final, but I can remember the goal vividly even though I haven't watched it a million times on video like some people think because I find it too embarrassing.

'Lee Dixon had played the ball up the line to Alan Smith who flicked it on, and when the ball came to me I remember thinking "I know what I'm going to do here" and that was to lob the ball over Steve Nicol, who was coming towards me, and run around him. It didn't quite go according to plan because my intended flick over the top of him actually clipped his shoulder and then hit me before going over Nicol, to leave me with a clear run on goal. I didn't know if there was anyone behind me, and I only had one thought in my head at that moment, which was to wait for Bruce Grobbelaar to make his move and then dink it over him.

'Sure enough, he went down and I knew exactly what I had to do. Thankfully my little chip went over him and into the net. The rest is a bit of a blur although I do remember trying to get up after I'd gone to ground and Martin Hayes grabbing me, almost breaking my neck in the process. The feeling of elation was incredible, and although I didn't know how long was left I knew there couldn't be much on the clock. Soon after that the final whistle went and it was party time. What a day; what a night.'

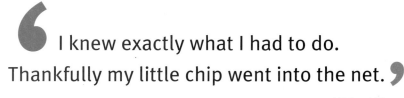

**I knew exactly what I had to do.
Thankfully my little chip went into the net.**

Michael Thomas

Dennis leaves Newcastle's Nikos Dabizas in a spin and clips the ball past Shay Given.

RUNNER-UP
Dennis Bergkamp v Newcastle
at St James' Park, FA Barclaycard Premiership, 2 March 2002
Michael Thomas's goal at Anfield was spectacular in its context, but Dennis
Bergkamp's sublime strike at St James' was memorable for its exquisite
execution. So good was Bergkamp's goal that several pundits doubted whether
his astonishing turn around United defender Nikos Dabizas was intended or
fortuitous. Dennis, however, soon confirmed that he knew exactly what he was
doing and was fully in control of the ball.

With his back to goal Dennis received a pass from Robert Pires but instead of
taking a touch to get the ball under control, the Arsenal striker met Pires's pass
with a delicious flick. The ball travelled to the left of Dabizas while Dennis moved
to the right, collecting it with a clear run at Shay Given's goal. Dabizas lunged and
missed, Given stepped forward but, as he did so, Dennis produced an accurate
side-foot finish into the corner of the net.

THIRD PLACE
Tony Adams v Everton
at Highbury, FA Carling Premiership, 3 May 1998
There is no more enduring image of the Arsenal's second 'double' than that of
Tony Adams soaking up Highbury's adulation after his goal against Everton in
May 1998. Although the fourth goal in the title-clinching victory, it was celebrated
so zealously that one might have been forgiven for thinking it was a late winner.

But this was a special goal scored by a player who had served Arsenal with a
loyalty and consistency rarely found in the modern game. Adams had picked up
the ball in his own half and after laying off a short pass to Steve Bould, he surged
forward into the Everton half. Bould, a player not renowned for his attacking play,
stepped forward and released an inch-perfect through ball. Collecting the pass,
Adams skipped into the Everton penalty area and crashed an unstoppable shot
past Thomas Myhre.

THE GREAT GAMES

Picking the three greatest games Arsenal have been involved in is not an easy task. Where to start? Where else but at Anfield on that dramatic night that ended with Michael Thomas's memorable goal – an overwhelming favourite of the fans who voted in the poll for this book.

WINNER

Liverpool 0 Arsenal 2
League title decider at Anfield, 26 May 1989
Even for a proud club steeped in history and success this was a special game. The facts were simple: first-placed Liverpool took on second-placed Arsenal in the season's concluding fixture, with the Londoners needing to win by two clear goals to claim the title for the first time in 18 years. The bad news for George Graham's team was that Liverpool hadn't lost at home by two goals since 1986, while Arsenal hadn't won at Anfield for 15 years.

At half time the score remained 0–0. Arsenal now had just 45 minutes to save their title dream. Seven minutes after the restart, Graham's team took the lead via an Alan Smith goal to give themselves hope. However, thereafter the game drifted towards the final whistle, with Liverpool seemingly destined to collect the title. But as the match moved into its 92nd minute, Michael Thomas took centre stage.

According to Thomas the 2–0 victory they needed was no more than they deserved and expected. 'From the start of that season, we felt we had a chance of winning the League,' Thomas recalls. 'We had so much confidence, so much self-belief and that year George Graham made us feel as though we were unbeatable. That's how we felt going up to Anfield, even though nobody else gave us a prayer.

'We weren't frightened about going up there as other teams were at the time and we always felt we were capable of winning. George had a plan too, which was to come in at half time 1–0 up and then score the winner in the last minute. It didn't quite happen like that, but it wasn't far off and the end result was exactly what we had envisaged. Even when it was 0–0 at half time we didn't panic, we still believed the title was ours. When Alan Smith scored after 52 minutes we knew it was.'

Then, of course, came a truly magical moment in Thomas's career. Brian Marwood missed the game through injury, but he recalls a defining moment which came long before either Smith's opener or Thomas's winner. 'I remember one incident early in the game which set the tone for the rest of the match. Tony Adams hit John Aldridge with a phenomenal challenge and from that moment on we were on top. But you still couldn't have scripted what happened after that.'

Liverpool: Grobbelaar, Ablett, Staunton, Venison, Nicol, Hansen, Houghton, Aldridge, Rush (Beardsley), Barnes, McMahon
Arsenal: Lukic, Dixon, Winterburn, Thomas, O'Leary, Adams, Rocastle, Richardson, Smith, Bould (Groves), Merson (Hayes)

That moment. Thomas mirrors the ecstasy of every Arsenal fan at Anfield.

RUNNER-UP

Arsenal 3 Manchester United 2, FA Cup final at Wembley Stadium, 12 May 1979
The last five minutes of the 1979 FA Cup final were extraordinary even by
Wembley standards. Yet such a dramatic climax had seemed unlikely when Frank
Stapleton made the score 2–0 before the break and Arsenal coasted through the
second half. But when United struck back with two late goals from McQueen and
McIlroy, it looked as if the game was heading for extra time. Liam Brady, though
utterly exhausted, had other ideas. Having already fashioned the opening two
goals, he released Graham Rix, whose pinpoint cross found Alan Sunderland, who
finished with a flourish past Gary Bailey, and the Cup was on its way to Highbury.
Arsenal: Jennings, Rice, Nelson, Talbot, O'Leary, Young, Brady, Sunderland,
Stapleton, Price (Walford), Rix
Manchester United: Bailey, Nicholl, Albiston, McIlroy, McQueen, Buchan, Coppell,
J. Greenhoff, Jordan, Macari, Thomas

THIRD PLACE

Manchester United 0 Arsenal 1, Premiership decider at Old Trafford, 8 May 2002
After beating Chelsea in the FA Cup final, Arsenal strode purposefully into Old
Trafford to claim the Club's third League and Cup 'double', thanks to a second-half
strike from Sylvain Wiltord on his 100th Arsenal appearance. It was a fitting
climax to a remarkable season for Arsène Wenger's men as they achieved their
12th successive League win, ensuring that they would end the season without an
away defeat and extending their record of scoring in every game of the campaign.
Manchester United: Barthez, P. Neville, Blanc, Brown, Silvestre, Scholes, Keane,
Veron (van Nistelrooy), Giggs, Solskjaer, Forlan (Fortune)
Arsenal: Seaman, Lauren, Campbell, Keown, Cole, Parlour, Vieira, Edu, Ljungberg,
Kanu (Dixon), Wiltord.

PLAYERS' SELECTIONS

Nigel Winterburn's All Time Arsenal XI
David Seaman, Lee Dixon, Steve Bould, Tony Adams, Kenny Sansom, Freddie Ljungberg, Patrick Vieira, Emmanuel Petit, Marc Overmars, Dennis Bergkamp, Thierry Henry.

Alan Skirton's All Time Arsenal XI
David Seaman, Lee Dixon, Martin Keown, Tony Adams, Peter Storey, George Armstrong, Patrick Vieira, Liam Brady, Robert Pires, Joe Baker, Thierry Henry.

Joe Baker's All Time Arsenal XI
Jack Kelsey, Martin Keown, Tony Adams, Frank McLintock, Thierry Henry, George Eastham, Dennis Bergkamp, Liam Brady, George Armstrong, Ian Wright, John Radford.

Charlie Nicholas's All Time Arsenal XI
Pat Jennings, Lee Dixon, Tony Adams, David O'Leary, Kenny Sansom, David Rocastle, Patrick Vieira, Liam Brady, Robert Pires, Thierry Henry, Dennis Bergkamp.

Chris Whyte's All Time Arsenal XI
Pat Jennings, Viv Anderson, David O'Leary, Tony Adams, Kenny Sansom, George Armstrong, Patrick Vieira, Liam Brady, Graham Rix, Ian Wright, Frank Stapleton.

John Radford's All Time Arsenal XI
Jack Kelsey, Peter Storey, David O'Leary, Tony Adams, Kenny Sansom, Robert Pires, Patrick Vieira, Liam Brady, George Armstrong, Charlie George, Thierry Henry.

Charlie George's All Time Arsenal XI
Pat Jennings, Lee Dixon, Tony Adams, Frank McLintock, Kenny Sansom, Robert Pires, Patrick Vieira, Liam Brady, Marc Overmars, Thierry Henry, Ian Wright.

Frank McLintock's All Time Arsenal XI
Pat Jennings, Pat Rice, Tony Adams, Peter Simpson, Kenny Sansom, Freddie Ljungberg, Patrick Vieira, Liam Brady, George Armstrong, Dennis Bergkamp, Thierry Henry.

Stewart Houston's All Time Arsenal XI
Pat Jennings, Lee Dixon, Tony Adams, Frank McLintock, Kenny Sansom, George Armstrong, Patrick Vieira, Liam Brady, Robert Pires, John Radford, Ian Wright.

Steve Williams' All Time Arsenal XI
Pat Jennings, Viv Anderson, Tony Adams, Frank McLintock, Kenny Sansom, David Rocastle, Patrick Vieira, Liam Brady, Cliff Bastin, John Radford, Ian Wright.

Kenny Sansom's All Time Arsenal XI
Pat Jennings, Lee Dixon, Tony Adams, Frank McLintock, Bob McNab, George Armstrong, Patrick Vieira, Liam Brady, Graham Rix, Ian Wright, Ted Drake.

Bob Wilson's All Time Arsenal XI
David Seaman, Lee Dixon, Frank McLintock, Tony Adams, Kenny Sansom, Robert Pires, Patrick Vieira, Liam Brady, George Armstrong, Dennis Bergkamp, Thierry Henry.

Alan Ball's All Time Arsenal XI
Jack Kelsey, Don Howe, Frank McLintock, Peter Simpson, Kenny Sansom, George Armstrong, Joe Mercer, Patrick Vieira, Robert Pires, Thierry Henry, Malcolm Macdonald.

8jbmaughan
97riccon
a17ocdi
Abdia Haaji, Yuusuf
Abimbola, Sean Moses
Adam, Nik
afctone
Al-Muhammad, Ayham
alanandnicolle
Allen, Fraser
Allen, Maurice
Allen, Michael Royston
Anastasi, Carl
Andersen, Espen
Anderson, Eric
Anderson, Ross
andyas64
Anjos, Michael
Anscombe, Mike
Antino, Paul
Anyole, Joel
Arlen, Dean
Armitt, Lee
Army, Paul
Arnold, Ron
Aslett
Astle, Julian
Aston, Louise
Augustine, Rutaganda
Ayres, David
Aziz, Pirmohamed
Azmi, Ahmad
Bacon, Michael
Bajwa, Raazi
Baker, David
Baldwin, John
Baldwin-Smith, Ashley
Bank of Friendship, June,
   Rose & Fudge
Barbic, David
Barker, Paul
Barnes, Brian
Barrow, Nicolas
Barton, Joe
basik
Batchelor, Jason
Bates, Paul
Batten, Neil
Beckman, Erik
Begg, Matt
Behan, Shaun
Benn, Philip
Bergkamp, A R J
Bergkamp, Dennis
Berry, Frank
Berry, Jason
Berry, Nathan
Bestwick, Rob
bigbother1
Biggadike, Matthew
Biggadike, Russell
Binder, John
Bjarkason, Johann
Bjerkeflata, Stian
Blackburn, G
blackmatch

Blair, Marc
Blake, Alex James
Blake, Russell James
Blau, Michael
blokeybonce
Bob, Tilly
Bobbett, Mick
Bolin, Goran
Borg, Anders
Borra, John
Boss, Andy
Boswell, Jolene
Boulton, Richard
Bowler, Peter
Bragger, Mat
Brass, Anthony
Brewer, Daniel
Briffa, Bernie
Briffa, Jessica
Brindle, Mark
Brittain, William
Brown, Irena
Brown, Jonathan
Brown, Richard
Bruce, Nicholas
Bruce, Richard
Buckley, Philip
Bumann, John
Burgess, Simon
Burke, Terry
Burn, George
Burnell, Colin
Burton, Jonathan
Bush, Colin
Butlin, Dave
Byrne, Ian
Byrne, Nigel
Campbell, Scott
Campling, Lee
Cannon, Patrick
Cardew, Alan
Carter, Phil
Chajet, Gary
Challinor, Gary
Chamberlain, Steve
Champness, Steve
Charalambous, Soteris
Chavoush, Mick
Cheeseman, Peter
Cheuk, Simon
Cheungkapo
Chick, David
Chipchase, Louis
Chong, William
Chris, Dowd
Chrysanthou, James
Church, Robert
Ciaran, Lally
Clarke, Paul
Clement, Nick
Clemmins, J
clifftuss
Clover, Jason
Clutton, Robert
Cohen, Joseph
Coleman, Daniel

Coleman, Paul
Coles, Ian
Coles, Tristan
colleen
Collins, Alex
Comley, Keith
Conroy, Hugh
Conway, Clive
Coombes, Thomas
Cooper, Gary
Cooper, Neale
Cope, Peter
Corbett, Kevin
Cornwell, Sean
Cotterell, Barrie
Coulter, Darryl
Cox, Tony
craigy127csf
Craze, David
Crowhurst, Hayley
cspang2001hk
Culley, Jon
Culling, Bryan
Culver, Martin
Cumming, Neil
curtisad2002
cuteboyjoe22
daddyk
Dallender, Mickey
dapo166
Darkin, Robert
Davies, Gareth
Davis, Malcolm
Davis, Roger
Dawes, Brian
Deasy, John
Decatris, Phil
Dehle, Erik
Deltort, Nicolas
Dempsey, Gary
Deol, Amandeep
Devall, Paul
Dillin, Eric
djsammy
dlnypaul
Dobbs, Steven
Donaldson, Warren
Donnelly, Stuart
Doyle, Ian
Drummond, Alvin
Duncan, David A
Dunn, Campbell
Earwaker, James
edgars
Egan, David
Egan, Martin
Egholm, Hannis
Eke, Oly
El-Khoumisti, Faysal
Elguezabal, Martin
Elguezabal, Paul
Ellis, Theo
Ellis, Warren
Elsey, Simon
en Adam, Petra
eva831222

Evans, Gareth
Evans, Richard
Fahad
Farolan, Edward
Farrell, Mark
Fay, Richard
Featley, Daniel
Feest, Michael
Feller, David
Fenn, Chris
Few, Jonathan
Fidan, Dogan
Finch, Leon
Fisher, Donna
Fitch, Queen
Flanagan, Ray
Flavio, Luciani
Fletcher, D
Floyd, David
Flynn, Marc
Forrest, Gavin
Foster, Nigel
Fowler, David
Fowler, Stephen
Fraser, Sean
Freedman, Joshua
Freeth, Alexander
Frommer, David
Frost, Andrew
Froud, Tony
Fu, Lee Kwan
Fung, Lam
Galloway, James
Gamby, Tony
Gardner, Angela
gary
geir.hansen
Geopolus, Andrew
Georgopoulos, Andrew
Giaever-Enger, Nicholas
giannico
Gibbs, Jon
Gibbs, Roy
Gilbert, Mark
Gilder, Robert James
Gilland, Lee
gilospices
Gluckman, Jonathan
Goh, Alex
Goh, Alex
Gold, Eddie
Goodenough, Daniel
Goodman, John
Goodworth, Edward
Gooner, Stokey
Gordon, Neil
Gottesman, Sandi
Gowans, Martin
Grant, Colin
Grant, Donald
Greally, John
Green, Michael
Greene, Philip
Gregory, John
Gregory, Matthew
Grialg, Steven

Griffin, Henry
Griffin, Mick
Griffin, Perry
Griffiths, Robert
Gristwood, Andrew
Gross, Paul
Grossman, Dan
Gunn, Benn
Gunner, Mat
Gunnlaugsson, Yngvi
Hager, Robin
Hai, Walid
Hall, Tom
Halpin, Mark
Hammans, Lois
Hammond, Mark
Hanafi, Ali
Hannonen, Timo
Hanson, Alan
Hare, Steve
Harries, Ron
Harris, Claire
Harris, Donna
Harris, Jeffrey
Harris. Donna
Harvey, Leung Yu Hang
Harvey, William
Hawtin, Del
Hayes, Carl
Heard, Peter
Heath, Michael
Henry, Lewis
Hernaman, Ronnie
Herson, Mark
Hibbert, Colin
Hickey, Kenneth
Hicks, Adam G
Hicks, Luke Andrew
Hilditch, Stephen
Hill, Steven
hillsey71
Ho, Choi Pak
Ho, Joe
Ho, KaHung
Hodge, Richard
Hook Family, The
Hookway, Andrew
Horastead, Tony
Howard, Matthew
Hudson, Chris
Hughes, Barry
Huitson, Lloyd
Hunt, John
Hunter, James
Huseyin, Hakan
Hutchinson, Mark
ianc999
Ibbetson, Peter
icemanles
Jackson, Mark
Jacobs, Ian
Jacobs, Mark
Jacobs, Sam
James, B
James, C A
James, Chris

James, Daniel
Jameson, Yacks
Jamieson, Richard
Jarman, Stuart
Jay, Norman
Jenkins, Chris
Jenkins, Dave
Jensen, Paal Georg
Jerrams, P
Johansen, Zacharia
Johansson, Fredrik
Johnson, Jeremy
Johnson, Martin
Johnson, Paul
Jones, Gareth
Jones, Henry
Jones, Ian
Jones, Johnathan
Jones, Michael
Jones, Robert
Jorgensen, Martin
Joseph, Teggy
Jubon, Jamie
Judd, Tony
k72968, Dennis
Kakkonen, Petteri
Kakouris, George
Kan, Tin Lok
Karlsson, Johan
kborbk
Kedge, Robert
Keeble, Phill
Kekeke, Gare
Kelly, John
Kelsey, Peter
Kent, J
Khan, Atif
Kiarie, Mark
Kimber, Daniel
King, R P A
King, Sue
King, Yves Niyitegeka
Kingaby, Andrew
Kirby, Terry
Kirwan, Lar
Kit, Chan Cheuk
knockchreeboy
Knowles, Ian
Koko, Emmanuel
koso1
Krishnan, Raj
Kugonza, Kenneth
Kula, She
Kwapong, Marian
Lam, Liu Tsz
Lambert, John
Lambert, Richard
Lane, Graham
Lawler, James
Lawler, John
Lawson, Sabita
Leather, Bradley
Lee, Kent
Lee, Peter
Leeds, Bob
Leer, Kristian

leilei528leilei
Leong, Lian Koh
Leung, Aaran
Levermore, Alan
Levitt, James
Liddiard, Paul
lifes_a_bich28
Lillseven, Eivind
Linton, Shaun
Lister, Douglas
Livni, Aviad
Locke, Mark
Lockett, Gerald
Luke, Ricky
Lundberg, Gert
Macnamara, David
Magoo. Jimmy
Mallard, Steve
Maltz, Justin
Manchester, Luke
Manchester, Sam
Mancktelow, Paul
Manel, Paul
manfred1025
Mannings, Cornell
Maple, Vince
marsylnic
Martin, Nathan
Masenge, Maurice
Maslen, Darren
Mason, Alan
Mason, Sam
Massen, Simon
Matthews, Warren
McBain, Ed
McCann, Thomas
McCarron, Danny
McDonagh, Ronan
McEwan, Brian
Mcgrath, Finbar
McIntyre, Guy
McKay, Sam
McKay, Tony
McKee, Conor
McLaughlin, Vince
McLean, Fran
McPherson, Stuart
McPhillips, David
McPhillips, Patrick
Meier, James
Metcalf, Ian
Miccio, Fabrizio
Michael, Harry
Michael, Theo
Mikol, Jack
Milburn, Nigel
Milligan, Gavin
Minick, Edward
Moore, Andy
Moore, Peter
Moriarty, Terry
Morley, Lee
Moroney, Alma
Morris, Geoff
Morris, Jeremy
Morris, Steve

Morton, David
Moshir-Fatemi, Reza
Mounsey-Thear,
    Christopher
Mulligan, Aidan
Mulryan, Gareth
Munro, Tola
Murphy, Ben
Murphy, Craig
Murphy, James
Murray, David
Murray, Paul
Mushamu, Elias
Musyoki, Benjamin
Myhre, Alexander
Nakasuwan, Nut
Naphtal, Cleopas
Nasholm, Thomas
Natarajan, Shreedhar
Nathan, Mark
ncsuga
Neill, Andy
Newkey-Burden, Chas
Newland, Lawrence
Newman, Daniel
Newman, Kevin
Nicholls, Andy
Nichols, Simon
Nickolson, Stuart
Nicolaescu, Dan
Norris, Paul
Norton, Peter
nukem304
Nunn, Bradley
Nutman, Doron
Nuttman, Graham
O'Bryan, R
O'Farrell, Peter
O'Flaherty, Kevin
O'Gorman, M
O'Riordan, Paul
O'Sullivan, Austin
Oatridge, Nic
Ody, James
Oliver, David
Oliver, Eddie
Olufisibe, Feyi
Oppong, William
Orholm, Arild
Osborn, Peter
Osbourne, Jamie
Owen, Dave
Owen, David
Owen, Neil
Owusu, Jason
Packer, Stuart
Padmore, Thomas
Panayiotou, L
Panch, Rajpaul
Pari, Dinesh
Parr, Roger
Parris, Robert
Parry, Doug
Parsons, Peter
patsy2929
Patton, Dominic

List of Voters

Paul, Army
pberg
Peacock, Arron
Pearson, Neil
Pecqueur, Steven
Peddie, David
Penn, Ronald
Peyton, Miles
Pike, Alastair
Piper, Karen
Piper, Ron
Piper, Ronnie
Pittarides, Das
plectrumknight
Pollard, Geoff
Poly Friends, Bill
Pounds, C F
Pounds, Steven
Price, Dan
Price, Graham Anthony
Pucino, Felice
Puzzi, Roberto
Quinn, Adrian
Rathbone, Martin
Rawle, Rick
Reading, Gabriella
Reading, James
Reardon, Gavin
Reilly, F
Ren, Ang Kuan
Rensmoen, Dag
Reuben, James
Richards, John
Richardson, Steve
Roast, W
Roberts, C S
Roberts, John
Roberts, Phillip
Robertson, Andrew
Robertson, Paul
robgord2000
Robson, Matthew
Rodriguez, Fernando
Rooney, Robert
Root, James
Rosendaal, Rian
Routh, Ashley
Rowe, Nick
Rowling, Henry
Ruane, Declan
Rundle-East, Liam
Saheba, Sheba
Salomski, Jyrki
Sampurno, Hadi
Samson, Nigel
Samuels, Graham
Sandberg, Richard
Sarfo-Annin, Jason
Sargent, Kevin
Sargent, Paul
Savage, David
Say, Tony
Scarbocci, Paolo Haaland
Schlagman, Mike
Scott, Ian
Scott, Stuart

sectionjj
Serghi, Paul
Setford, Christopher
Seymour, Graeme
Shalamberidze, Levan
Shambi, Jaspal Singh
Shanwei, Fu
Shaw, Daniel
Shean, Tony
Sheldon, Stuart
Shenton, Dai
Shepherd, Robert
Sheriff, Oshy
Shillingford, Thomas
Sigward, Marco
Simmonds, G T
Simoen, Anthony
Sims, Robert
Simson, Steve
Sinko, Jumi
Skinner, Paul
Slattery, Mick
Smart, James
Smart, Matthew
Smart, Nick
Smith, Francis
Smith, Gary
Smith, Kerry
Smith, Michael Thomas
Smith, Tracey
soccertmt2
Soo, Jason
Southgate, Clive
Spencer, Edward
Spindler, Gerry
Spriggs, Richard
Springer, Paul
Stagrum, Espen
Steer, Richard
Stenman, Mattias
stephen
Stephenson, Roger
steve7
steveo_10_
sticky869
Stonham, Henry
Strong, Eric
Styles, Billy
Styles, Peter
sue
Sung, Nathanial
superflyflynn
supert54
Sutton, Dominic
Swain, Gerry
Talbott, Ross
Tam, Dennis
Tango, Lee
Taylor, James
Taylor, Mark
Taylor, Paul
Taylor, Tim
Teague, G
Teck, Kian
Teitsson, Eggert
Thatcher, Shane

Thaunthong, Phairuch
Theobald, Louise
Thomas, Michael
Thomson, Sean
Thorn, Bruce
Thorp, Martine
Ting, Steward
tingting195
To, Samuel
Tobin, Seamus
Tolson, Dickon
Tonkin, Robert
Torarenni, Jan
Tsang, Stephen
Tsatsas, Nicholas
Turkic, Zvjezdan
Turner, Neil
twilightsky
Twist, Steve
Ugochukwu,
    Chukwuemeka
Umoh, Iboro
Upham, Gerald
userb62
van Beeck-Nonboe, Joost
van Reenen, Bennet
Van Son, Bach
Vaughton, Michael
Vella, Johann
Vieira, Patrick
Viitanen, Petri
Vito-Cruz, Mark Alvin
Voice, Jonathan
Voituret, Tony
Wadey, Kevin
Wakeling, Greg
Wakerly, George
Walker, Derek
Walker, J S
Walters, Anthony
Waltham, Gary
Ward, Alex
Ward, Dean Darren
Ward, Nathan
Ward, Paul
Ward, Peter
Ward, Ray
Warne, Valentino
Wasiu, Fagbenro
Waters, Joe
Watkins, Matthew
Watkins, Sam
Watts, Martin
Watts, Ray
Webb, Lee
Webster, Allan
Webster, John
Wenbourne, Nick
Wend, John
West, Trevor
Westwood , Mark
Whenman, Brenda
White, Andrew
White, Dan
White, Grant
White, Phil

Whitenker, Ronald
Whiting, Gavin
Wibe, Christer
Wigmore, D
Wiik, Magnus
wildting260386
Wilks, Jonathan
Williams, Christopher
Williams, Paraic
Williams, Terence
Willimott, Roger John
Wills, A
Wilson, Ray
Wilson, S D
Winfield, Joshua
Winfield, Roger
Wing-M, Chan
Winn, Kurtis-Daniel
Wolfson, Neil
Wong, Andy
Wong, Belinda
Wong, Siu-Kei
Wood, Andrew
Wood, Jonathan
Wooler, Daniel
Wootton, Donald James
Wootton, Mark James
Wray, John
Wyatt, Bryan
yeeinfo
Ying, Liu
yiuchoi
Young, SimonYuen, Mr
Zienkowicz, Mark

Index

Acknowledgements

Photographic acknowledgements in source order:

Arsenal Football Club plc 9, 10, 11, 17, 22, 23, 27, 29, 33, 44, 46, 47, 49, 51, 52, 56, 68, 70, 71, 72, 75, 79, 80, 92, 93, 106, 107, 109, 111, 113, 115, 116, 118, 119, 121, 122, 124, 127, 130, 131, 133, 135, 140, 142, 143, 151 top left, 151 top right, 151 bottom right, 151 bottom left, 151 centre right top, 151 centre right bottom, 151 centre left top, 151 centre left bottom
Colorsport 4, 7, 13, 15, 19, 20, 21, 25, 31, 32, 34, 35, 37, 39, 40, 43, 46 top, 46 bottom, 55, 58, 59, 61, 63, 64, 67, 77, 81, 82, 83, 85, 87, 89, 91, 94, 95, 97, 99, 101, 103, 104, 105, 117, 128, 129, 137, 139, 141, 147, 149, 153

Acknowledgements
The authors would like to thank the following people for their help at various stages of this book's production. Firstly Trevor Davies and Jessica Cowie at Hamlyn for their patience and assistance throughout; Joe Cohen and Andy Exley at Arsenal; and the former Arsenal players who gave their time so generously – particular thanks go to Viv Anderson, Liam Brady, Paul Davis, Brian Marwood, Niall Quinn and Michael Thomas.

Bibliography
Adams, Tony with Ridley, Ian, *Addicted*, Collins Willow, 1998
Barrett, Norman S., *Purnell's New Encyclopedia of Association Football*, Purnell, 1972
Hugman, Barry J., *The PFA Premier and Football League Players' Records 1946–1998*, Lenard Queen Anne Press, 1998
Joyce, Michael, *Football League Players' Records 1888–1939*, SoccerData Publications, 2002
Pires, Robert, *Footballeur: An Autobiography*, Vintage/Ebury, 2002
Ponting, Ivan, *Arsenal Player by Player*, Hamlyn, 2001
Soar, Phil and Tyler, Martin, *The Official Arsenal History*, Hamlyn, 2002

The following yearbooks and periodicals also proved extremely useful in the research for this book:
The Official Arsenal magazine
The Arsenal matchday programme
The Rothmans Football Yearbook
The PFA Footballers' Who's Who

Celebrity selections
The celebrity selections in this book are based on material from a series of articles written by Colin Benson for the Arsenal matchday programme.

Executive Editor: **Trevor Davies**
Project Editor: **Jessica Cowie**
Executive Art Editor: **Joanna MacGregor**
Designer: **Darren Southern**
Picture Manager: **Liz Fowler**
Senior Production Controller: **Jo Sim**